Hell Fire
DAMNATION

Maurice J. G. Stevens

authorHOUSE

AuthorHouse™ UK
1663 Liberty Drive
Bloomington, IN 47403 USA
www.authorhouse.co.uk
Phone: 0800.197.4150

© 2017 Maurice J. G. Stevens. All rights reserved.

No part of this book may be reproduced, stored in a retrieval system, or transmitted by any means without the written permission of the author.

Published by AuthorHouse 04/18/2017

ISBN: 978-1-5246-6776-4 (sc)
ISBN: 978-1-5246-6777-1 (hc)
ISBN: 978-1-5246-6775-7 (e)

Print information available on the last page.

Any people depicted in stock imagery provided by Thinkstock are models, and such images are being used for illustrative purposes only.
Certain stock imagery © Thinkstock.

This book is printed on acid-free paper.

Because of the dynamic nature of the Internet, any web addresses or links contained in this book may have changed since publication and may no longer be valid. The views expressed in this work are solely those of the author and do not necessarily reflect the views of the publisher, and the publisher hereby disclaims any responsibility for them.

Scripture quotations marked KJV are from the Holy Bible, King James Version (Authorized Version). First published in 1611. Quoted from the KJV Classic Reference Bible, Copyright © 1983 by The Zondervan Corporation.

TABLE OF CONTENTS

HELL FIRE AND DAMNATION!.............. 1

THE BIBLE ACCORDING TO MAURICE! 7

IS RELIGIOUS BELIEF REALLY NECESSARY?....................... 73

CLASSICAL MUSIC ACCORDING TO MAURICE! 113

MY RECOLLECTIONS OF BRITISH POLITICAL LIFE SINCE 1939. 155

THE SIMPLE SOLUTION TO POVERTY AND POPULATION EXPLOSION!...................................... 173

MY SEQUAL TO TOM BROWN'S SCHOOL DAYS................................. 181

A TREMENDOUS TRIUMPH OVER GREAT ADVERSITY 217

SECOND THOUGHTS! 233

MY LIFE'S MEMORIES 237

BIBLE STORY REFERENCE:............. 267

HELL FIRE AND DAMNATION!

I was a complete failure at school. My English skills were abysmal. However I seemed to have been blessed with a very good memory with very good and clear logical thinking skills. I have never found a clever Christian Leader who was able to undermine the great clarity of my logical reasoning!

The wide-spread misconception by the public is that Christianity was most likely to be good and honourable. They rightly perceive Jesus to be a very good man as I believe Him to be. However I believe this gross public error of judgement is due to centuries of insidious and unremitting propaganda by the Church. This is from the highest and most respected echelons of society.

The misguided story goes like this. It is claimed that God cannot tolerate the slightest sin or imperfection, and that He is compelled to punish it severally. I contend, on the other hand that this is very strange, and unbelievable, as God knew very well before He commenced on His creation of mankind, that people would be always afflicted with the malaise of imperfection. The Bible recounts that all have sinned and come short of the glory of God! I feel that almighty God would be most uncomfortable living side by side with us in all our imperfection. We were, however, created in His own image for His companionship. There is no end to the difficulties of Christian belief!

Hell is a major embarrassment to Christian believers. God is continually portrayed as a God of great love, mercy, and forgiveness. Slow to anger and plenteous in mercy. Not wishing anyone to perish. The Christian Church today, rarely ever mentions their great difficulty of a belief in Hell. It is claimed that God before creation made a plan of salvation for mankind in the cruel death, and great sacrifice of His dear Son. On the surface this sounds the perfect answer to Christian Faith. However, as is usually the case, all is never plain sailing! It is perfectly clear that only a small minority of humanity will avail themselves of this salvation plan. The Bible says that narrow is the gate, and straight is the way that leadeth onto salvation, and few there be that find it! So there! God plan is an unmitigated failure isn't?

In human justice Judges apportion a penalty that fits the crime. God, on the other hand, in His wisdom, shows no discernment between gross and minor crimes or sins. He suffers from a melodramatic obsession with total, and as He knows very well, impossible perfection!

I believe that most people leading their lives to the very best of their ability, bringing up their children with love, and devotion, do not deserve to be sent to Hell for eternity to suffer terrible torment, and as the Bible graphically puts it, 'There will be weeping and gnashing of teeth.' Very strong language indeed! Only God Himself could have dreamed up such a draconian punishment as eternal terrible suffering. It would have been totally beyond the power, and conception of evil men!

My dear readers, do I really need to say any more to you? Surely my case against organised Christianity has been proved beyond any doubt at all?!

THE BIBLE ACCORDING TO MAURICE!

The Bible is crammed-packed with the most amazing and best stories ever written! I propose to recount them in a concise, interesting and easy to read manner. To my knowledge this has never been achieved before. I commend my writing to non-believers and believers alike, and to young children.

Let's begin. Here we go. The first book of the Bible is called Genesis. This was believed to have been written by Moses. The first page is the story of God's creation of all things. This was achieved in the record breaking time of six days! God rested on the seventh day. I should think so!

His triumph in creation was man, created in God's own image called Adam. The Bible says that God communed with Adam in the cool of the day. God felt that Adam may need companionship, so he put him into a deep sleep. He then removed one of Adam's ribs and miraculously created Eve.

All was well until the Devil in the guise of a serpent tempted Adam and Eve to disobey God and to eat the forbidden fruit, gaining them the knowledge of good and evil. They then realised that they were naked and sowed fig leaves to cover up their private parts. God confronted them about their disobedience, and said to them, "Who told you that you were naked?" Adam in his defence told God that Eve had led him astray. Women have been blamed for this throughout history.

God banished them from the idyllic Garden of Eden. An Angel was stationed at the entrance to the Garden with a flaming sword to prevent their return.

Adam and Eve had to adjust to living in a 'Fallen' world complete with thorns and thistles. The Garden of Eden was thought to be near the river Euphrates. As with nature Adam and Eve procreated and had two sons Cain and Able. Cain tilled the soil for produce, while Able kept flocks of sheep. It was felt that a sacrifice was necessary to appease Almighty God. Able found favour with God by offering up in a sacrifice a lamb. Cain on the other hand displeased God by offering up some of the fruits of his labours.

This led to brotherly enmity, and Cain killed his brother Able. God put a mark on Cain's forehead so that everyone who met him would try to kill him. Cain said that his punishment was greater than he could bear. Life went on and the Bible says that men of the world saw that the daughters of men were fair, and took everyone a wife!

Let us move on in the book of Genesis to a patriarch called Abraham. He was the father of both the Jewish and Arab races. He lived in the city of Ur. God called him to leave the city, and he became a nomad and lived in a tent. His wife was called Sarah. God surprisingly promised Abram to make a great nation out of his stock. However there was an insuperable difficulty as Sarah was barren.

Surprisingly Abram carried on in his faith in God. This seemed to be a wise move as eventually Sarah conceived and bore a son called Isaac. Life is never plain sailing as God called Abram to offer up a sacrifice to Him. He went on a long journey with his son Isaac. They reached the destination, and Abram built an altar. Isaac understandably asked his father where the sacrifice was. Abram replied wryly that God would provide the sacrifice.

However he then laid Isaac on the altar and raised his knife to kill his only son. God intervened, and told Abram to stop. God said to Abram, "Now I know that you love me!" God then provided the sacrifice as Abram looked around and saw a lamb caught up in a thicket. He duly sacrificed the lamb to his God.

Isaac had to travel into a far country to find his bride Rebecca. Their union produced two sons, Jacob and Esau. He is the father of the Arabs. One day Esau had been hunting, and came back home very hungry. Scheming Jacob presented Esau with a very hard choice. He asked his brother if he would sell his birth right for a mess of potage. Esau's stomach got the better of him and he agreed.

Isaac was a very old man, nearly blind. It was the right time to give his blessing to his eldest son Esau. Jacob known in the Bible as the Great Deceiver tricked his brother out of his birth right by putting hairy skins on his arms to deceive his father into thinking it was his brother's hairy arms. Isaac said the voice is that of Jacob but the arms are of Esau. He then gave Jacob his blessing.

Jacob left the security of his home for fear that his brother Esau would kill him. One night alone he lay down to sleep with a stone for a pillow. He saw a ladder reaching up into Heaven with Angels ascending and descending. An Angel wrestled with him all night. When the terrible ordeal of the night was over, God said to Jacob, "You will no longer be known as Jacob but Israel." The

Jewish state is known by this name even today!

Jacob looked for some work. A man known as Laban gave him employment. During the next seven years Jacob fell in love with one of Laban's two daughters Rachel. Her sister was Leah. Jacob was then allowed to marry who he thought was the love of his life Rachel. However this was not to be. Laban tricked Jacob into giving him Leah instead. He never found any love for her. Jacob must have been unkindly reminded of his great deception of his brother Esau. Laban made Jacob work for another seven long years before consenting for Jacob to marry Rachel. What men do for love!

Jacob, Rachel and Leah had twelve sons. They had been really busy! The oldest was Ruben, and the youngest was Benjamin.

Joseph was the second youngest and the most favourite son. The Bible says that Jacob favoured him by giving him a very expensive coat of many colours. Joseph was a dreamer. His brothers naturally hated their father's favourite child. His dreams were many. One that annoyed his brethren greatly was that he dreamt that the moon and stars bowed down to him.

One day his father asked him to go and look for his brothers who had gone a great distance with their flocks of sheep to find pasture. When his brothers saw him a long way off, they said to each other, "Let us kill him." Ruben more responsibly said, "Let us not kill him for he is our brother." They then decided to lower Joseph into a deep well. Ruben hoped to rescue him later on.

A travelling group of Ishmaelite's traveling to Egypt attracted the brother's attention. They sold Joseph for money, and killed a lamb to sprinkle its blood on Joseph's coat of many colours. When they returned home they showed their father the blood stained coat. Jacob was convinced and said, "A wild beast must have devoured him.

The Ishmaelite's sold Joseph into slavery, in Egypt. An important man called Potiphar bought him. Joseph decided wisely to make the best of his most difficult situation. He was an able and very conscientious slave. He had the great advantage in life of having good looks. The Bible puts it in a lovely way, and says he was of ruddy countenance! Potiphar made him in charge of his entire house. Potiphar's wife fancied him, and one day in her bedroom she tried to entice him into love making. Joseph was having nothing to do with this, and fled leaving his coat behind him. She then complained to Potiphar about Joseph's wrong doing. Potiphar was very angry and consigned Joseph to prison. Potiphar's wife showed her husband Joseph left coat as evidence against him.

Even this unjust calamity did not deter Joseph from exceling in all he did. The prison governor quickly realized that

Joseph was a man of ability and great talent, and promoted him to be in charge of all the other prisoners. One was Pharaoh's baker. He had a dream about what his fate would be. Joseph the gifted dreamer interpreted his dream, and told the baker that he would soon be released and would return to his former position as Pharaoh's chief baker.

This came to pass, but Joseph had asked him to bring to Pharaoh his unjust plight. The baker however forgot all about Joseph languishing in prison for many long years. Fortunately for Joseph Pharaoh had a dream which troubled him greatly. He dreamt that seven fat cattle eat up seven lean cattle. His sorcerers were baffled, and had no idea what the dream meant. The baker had a latter-day inspiration, and remembered Joseph in prison. He related to Pharaoh that Joseph had correctly interpreted his dream.

Pharaoh ordered that Joseph be released from prison, and brought before him. Joseph heart skipped a beat, and he changed his clothes and shaved. Before Pharaoh he correctly interpreted Pharaoh's dream. He said there would be seven years of good harvests followed by seven long years of famine. Pharaoh was so impressed by Joseph's amazing ability that he made Joseph second in command in all Egypt. Pharaoh said, "Who better than Joseph to make wise preparation for our future."

Joseph bought surplice grain from Egypt's farmers in the seven years of plenty. Then seeming disaster struck, and a terrible and prolonged famine ensued. People very short of food came and complained about their plight to Pharaoh. He told them to go to Joseph for their help. Joseph opened up the stores of grain and sold it to the people.

Jacob and his large family were not immune to the wide-spread famine. He heard that there was grain in Egypt. He sent his sons with money to buy grain, but he refused to let Benjamin his youngest son to go. The brothers arrived in Egypt and were directed to see Joseph. He recognised his brethren, but did not disclose this to them. He spoke roughly to them, and accused them of coming to spy out the land.

However the brothers were able to buy some sacks of grain which they paid Joseph for. On their long journey home Joseph sent his guards on horseback to stop his brethren. Their bags of grain were opened, and to the brother's great astonishment were the bags of money they had paid for the grain. They were all made to return to Egypt. Joseph said to them, "Wherefore have you come to rob me?"

Joseph told his brethren to go back home and return with his youngest brother Benjamin. When they arrived home they told Jacob of what was required. Jacob refused to let Benjamin leave; He said that his grey hairs would bring him in sorrow down to the grave if any calamity were to happened to his son. However the famine got the better of them, and Benjamin was allowed to go. Meanwhile Joseph had taken the wise precaution of detaining their brother Judah in prison as a hostage.

The brothers turned to each other and said this is God's punishment for the evil we did our brother Joseph. They did not realize that Joseph could understand all that they said to each other. Joseph left the room to weep with emotion. He returned to his brothers and said, "I forgive you. It was God's plan to save much life. Is my father still alive?" He embraced them each in turn.

Joseph told Pharaoh of all that had transpired. Pharaoh was so greatly impressed that he told Joseph to bring his father and family to come and live in the security of Egypt. They were given the most productive land in the country called the land of Goshen.

When Jacob saw the many waggons coming to take them all to Egypt, he remarked, "It is true Joseph my son that was dead is still alive!". When they all arrived at the Egyptian court Joseph embraced his beloved father, and in particular his brother Benjamin. Jacob blessed Pharaoh as was his custom in those days.

The family multiplied, and prospered in this land of plenty, so much so that the indigenous Egyptians became ever more wary of the new immigrants. This was not a dissimilar reaction of today in Europe where there is ever increasing concern by the public that too much immigration would lead to an unacceptable dilution of their own beloved country.

A new Pharaoh was now in power, who did not know Joseph or his background at all. An order was made to enslave Jacob's decedents, and they were dragooned into forced labour. One of their tasks was to make bricks for building out of clay. This process required some straw; however this was always in very short supply. They complained about this, but nothing was done about it. Their task-masters just made them work even harder.

One of the most draconian measures brought in by the Egyptian's was to kill all their first new born babies. The mother of Moses, however had, what turned out to be a very brilliant plan indeed! She hid baby Moses in a basket and obscured him from public view by hiding him in the bulrushes on the bank of the river Nile.

Great miracles never cease to happen in Bible stories, as Pharaoh's young daughter with her handmaidens found baby Moses. She was allowed to adopt him, and bring him up in Pharaoh's household, with all the privileges, and the noble education this allowed.

When Moses had reached adulthood, he became aware of his fellow countries men's plight. One day he saw a taskmaster beat one of his decedents, and Moses was so outraged that he killed the man. He was then compelled to leave the country for the sake of his own life.

After many years Moses returned to Egypt, and became his decedent's leader. However he had an impediment of stammering speech. His brother, Aron was a gifted public speaker. When God told Moses to go and speak on behalf of his people to Pharaoh for the release of his people from their terrible slavery, he replied to God that he felt he was not capable of this great task, because of his speech impediment, and that God should consider his capable brother instead.

However God usually knows best and Moses was instructed to negotiate his people's release from slavery with Pharaoh. Pharaoh refused, and Moses promised that plagues would follow his intransigence.

The first plague to afflict the Egyptians was a plague of locusts that devoured all green vegetation Moses returned again to Pharaoh in case he had changed his mind. Pharaoh changed his mind under great pressure and agreed to let Moses' people go. This did not happen, and Moses had to return several more times with further threats of more sinister plagues to follow. There was plague of frogs, followed by the river Nile turning red like blood. Finally God's patience expired and He sent an angel to kill all the first born Egyptians. Moses's people had to put a blood sign on the front of their doors, so the angel of the Lord would pass by. This led to the important custom of these people, of The Feast of the Passover.

Pharaoh patience had expired, and he agreed to let Moses's people to leave his country. After some time Pharaoh as was his habit, changed his mind yet again. He sent his elite chariot guard in pursuit of Moses and his people. God was always overlooking and as the Egyptians came near God cause a flood and swamp by an overflowing river to bog down the pursuers. Moses and his people miraculously crossed the river on dry land; The Egyptians were drowned as the river closed over them.

Jacob's twelve sons were the fathers' of the twelve tribes of Israel. Only the tribe of Judah survives today, as the other tribes intermarried, and lost their identity,

God continually watched over Moses's people with a bright display in the sky before them, showing them the way to go. Aron, Moses's brother became the High Priest. He was from the tribe of Levi. This was the priestly tribe that did not have to work, and were supported by gifts from the other tribes. The people built a Tabernacle to worship God in. It was a structure made out of a tent, with the Holy of Holies at the far end, sealed off with a curtain. The alter, the Arch of the Covenant, an ornate box containing the two tablets of stone on which God had written the Ten Commandments, together with Aron's rod which miraculously budded. On the top was a candlestick with seven candles.

Turning back to the Ten Commandments, they were given to Moses by God on a mountain top nearby. However Moses was away for a very long time indeed. His people did not know what had befallen their leader, or if he was even still alive. Aron who was temporally in charge was asked by the people to make a Golden Calf out of their jewellery they had obtained in their sojourn in captivity in Egypt. This was an ancient symbol of fertility.

Aron unwisely agreed to their request. When all was completed they all gathered together to worship it. It degenerated into a sexual orgy. The long away Moses returned from the mountain top, and to his great horror saw the great decadence of his people. He dropped the precious stones of the Commandments, and they shattered.

Moses people, Jacob's decedents, now known as the Israelites, after God gave Jacob a new name, had, as a punishment for their decadence, to delay their entry into the land of Canaan for forty years. Moses died during this time, and Joshua took over the leadership of the Israelites.

During these forty years they had multiplied and grown into a formidable force. This was necessary as the fortified city of Jericho lay in their path to the promised land of 'Milk and Honey!' The city had what seemed an impenetrable city wall.

Joshua and Caleb went to spy out the city. They came across some unexpected help from a prostitute called Rehab. Her home was situated on the wide city wall. She told the spies that their God was very powerful, and that her city would fall into their hands. Joshua and Caleb struck a deal with her, and promised her that she and all her family would be spared in the ensuing battle. As identification she was required to hang a scarlet rope from the top of the city wall at her home.

The Israelites formed up in a long column, with the Priests, the Arch, and trumpeters at the fore. The inhabitants must have wondered what was going on. They had to encircle the city seven times before the wall of the city miraculously fell down flat. God had told the Israelites to kill all the people they came across in the Promised Land of Canaan. They killed everyone except Rehab the Harlot and all her family as promised. Jesus was directly related to Rehab through the lineage of King David, who was related to Rehab. They took her, and all her family to live with them in the land of Canaan.

Samuel was their greatest prophet. During the time of the prophet Eli, Samuel a young boy was living with Eli. One night Samuel called out to Eli, and said, "Did you call me?! Eli replied that he had not. This happened again a few times until Eli perceived that it was God calling Samuel. He told Samuel to reply, "Here am I!"

The Israelites as time went by grew restless, and longed for a King to rule over them, instead of Samuel. Samuel warned them that a King would tax them, and use their men in battle. However the clamour for change was unabated. Samuel carried out the wishes of his people, and found a King for them. He chose Saul, a man head and shoulders above his countrymen.

Saul's reign was a very troubled one. He suffered from manic depression, and got a young boy called David to play the harp, as music has always had a soothing and calming effect on the mind. Samuel still had great influence in the land, and realized that a successor to Saul was required. He went to the house and family of Jessie. Samuel asked Jessie to line up all his sons so he could evaluate them. After passing down the assembled line he found none to his liking. He said to Jessie, "Are there any more sons?" Jessie thought a while and said there was his youngest son David, who was out tending the flocks of sheep, and would quickly summon him for Samuel to consider. David duly arrived and Samuel anointed his head with holy oil, as the next king of the Israelites.

Saul was always in trouble with the neighbouring Philistines. Their armies faced each other on the two sides of a hill with a brook at the bottom. Goliath, the Philistine's super human champion complete with a sword bearer mocked the Israelites, and taunted them to send one of their best solders to do combat with him. King Saul was the obvious first choice for this unenviable challenge. He did not accept. David, just a young man, told Saul that he would willingly fight this uncircumcised Philistine. Saul offered David his heavy armour to try on. David found it too heavy and unsuitable for combat. He told Saul that as his father's shepherd he had killed a lion attacking his sheep.

David with just a sling walked calmly down the side of the hill to the bottom where he found some small stones in the steam. He climbed the other side of the hill and drew near to confront Goliath. He mocked David to his great misfortune. David wielded his sling with a chosen stone and hurled it accurately so that the stone hit and sank deep into Goliath's scull. David then took Goliath's sword and duly cut off his head. In an exalted act of triumph he held the head aloft to the great delight of the Israelites on the other side of the hill. Their womenfolk, to the great annoyance of King Saul, sang that Saul had killed his hundreds but David had killed his thousands!

David succeeded Saul as king, and became their most successful warrior. His son Absalom conspired to overthrow David, and in the ensuing battle lost his life, as he was riding on horseback through a forest. His long hair was caught up in the branches of a tree, and he was hanged. David was, however, filled with remorse at the loss of his beloved son.

Uriah the Hittite's wife, Beersheba was extremely beautiful. This did not pass King David's attention. Like so often today, he lusted after her, so much so that he conspired to kill Uriah. This was not as simple as it seems. David arranged for Uriah to be sent to the front line of battle, so hopefully for David he would be killed. This happened, and David took Beersheba as his wife. They had a child that died. God's punishment for sin. Their second child Solomon became the richest and most wise King of Israel. David was not allowed by God to build the Jewish temple, as God said that he had spilt much blood in battle. This was left to King Solomon.

The Prophet came to see David, and recounted a grim story to him. He said that a very rich man had stolen a very poor man's only lamb. David was furious, and decreed that this man should be severely punished. In the most wonderful, concise, and very powerful words of The King James version of the Bible, the Prophet uttered these words, "Thou art the man"!

In the Book of Ruth, during the time of Israel's judges, there was a great famine in the land. A family from Bethlehem, Elimelech and his wife Naomi with their sons Mahlon and Chilion emigrated to the nearby country of Moab. Elimelech died, and his two sons married two Moabite woman. Mahlon married Ruth, and Chilion married Orpah.

After ten tears the two sons of Namoi died in Moab. Namoi decided to return to Bethlehem. She told her daughter's-in-law to return to their own country, and to remarry. Orpah reluctantly left, however Ruth said, "Entreat me not to leave thee, or to return from following after thee, wither thou goest, I will go, and where thou lodgest I will lodge. Thy people will be my people and thy God my God. Where thou doest die I will die, and there will I be buried."

Namoi and Ruth returned to Bethlehem at the beginning of the barley harvest, and in order to support her daughter-in-law and herself, Ruth went to the fields to glean. The corn fields belonged to a man called Boaz. He was kind to her as he had heard of her loyalty to her mother-in-law.

Boaz was a close relative of Naomi's husband's family. He was obliged by the Levirate law to marry Mahlon's widow

Ruth, in order to carry on his families' inheritance. Namoi sent Ruth to the threshing floor, and told her to go where he slept, and uncover his feet, and lay thee down, and he will tell thee what thou shalt do. Ruth did so. Some scholars interpret the uncovering of feet as a reference to the genitals.

At midnight Boaz was afraid, and turned to see that a woman lay at his feet. When she said who she was, she replied, "I am Ruth thy handmaid; spread therefore thy skirt over thine handmaid for thou art a near kinsman. Boaz blessed her, and agreed to do all she required, and noted that all the city of the people doth know that thou art a virtuous woman. Boaz married Ruth, and their son Obed was the father of Jessie, the father of King David, and related to Jesus.

The book of Ester is often associated with the book of Ruth. Ester is the only book in the Bible not to mention God! It was set in ancient Persia capital of Susa. The ruler at that time was Ahasuerus. His Queen was Vashti. Her cousin was Mordecai a Jew. He discovers a plot. Two courters Bigthen and Teresin were hanged.

Haman, the villain in the piece, was a Viceroy. He planned to kill Mordecai, and all the Jews in the empire. Mordecai understandably implores Vashti to intercede with the King. The law was that the Queen could not go and meet the King, unless summoned.

Mordecai ordered a fast for three days. Ester then draws enough courage to go to see the King. Fortunately the king held out his golden sceptre, and all was well. A feast is arranged in which Haman would be invited.

Haman is offended by Mordecai's wife, and prepares gallows to hang him. Meanwhile Ahasuerus is asked by Haman for permission to hang Mordecai. The King Askes Haman what should be done to honour the man the King regards. Smug Haman thinking he was to be honoured said, "The King should place the royal robes on his shoulders, and he should be paraded around the city. The Queen had persuaded Ahasuerus of the dastardly plot to kill her people. Haman was astounded to be told by the King, "Go and do all you have said to Mordecai the Jew.

Haman fell out of favour with the King, and was executed on the very same gallows as he had prepared for his enemy Mordecai. An order from the King made it possible for the Jewish community to seek revenge. It is thought that 70,000 Persians were slaughtered by the Jewish community.

The book of Job was a very ancient book indeed. God had blessed him with great earthly wealth, and many sons. Satan had perceived, wrongly, as it turned out, that the only reason Job loved his God was because of God's blessing. Evil Satan devised a plan of action to discover the real truth about Job. Meeting God Satan put his theory to God, and remarked that if God decided to take all Job's wealth and prosperity away from him, he would curse God.

Very surprisingly God agreed to this awful plan. Satan saw to it that Job lost all his wealth, and Job's servants reported to him that all his sons had perished. It did not stop there. Job's body was covered with sores, and he lay in ashes. Job's friends were obviously dismayed by all this misfortune, and wrongly concluded that Job must have sinned. They were known as Job's Comforters!

They tried in vain to persuade Job to curse God and die. The story concludes by recounting that Job refused to curse his God. Satan had failed in his evil plan, and that God's view of Job was the correct one. God then restored even more to Job than he had ever had before!

You would be quite rightly be forgiven for believing that the Holy Bible did not condone the partaking of sexual pleasure. However you would be terribly wrong! The book called The Song Of Solomon is a celebration of sexual love, pleasure and delight! The book is a unique insight into sexual love. The two participants rejoice in their sexual intimacy. It is an allegory of the relationship between God and Israel.

Next I am going to consider the book of Daniel. His name means 'God is my Judge.' It is an account of Daniel, and his three friends, Shadrach, Meshach, and Abednego. They were all Jewish nobility, and were taken into captivity during 605BC. It was in the third reign of Jehoiakim King of Juda that these four Israelites were taken into captivity by King Nebuchadnezzar of Babylon in Assyria.

As they were of Jewish nobility they were selected for special training for senior positions in the land. They were given special food to eat, including the King's meat. Daniel refused it as it had been offered to Idols. He chose rather to eat just a diet of pulses. However they grew in stature, and suffered no ill effects. Daniel would pray to his God each day, opening his widow which faces due east to his beloved Jerusalem which was never very far from his mind.

In the Babylonian Court King Belshazzar held a feast. During these festivities the King saw a hand writing on the wall. It is writing in a language the King was unable to understand. Daniel came to the rescue. He said that the writing said that his kingdom would be given to the Medes and Persians.

Somehow Daniel and his three friends fell out of favour with the King, and Daniel was thrown into The Den of Lions! However God sent an Angel to shut up the lion's mouths, and Daniel came to no harm. His three friends were subjected to a far worse fate. The King ordered that the Fiery Furnace be heated seven times hotter than usual. Meshach, Shadrach, and Abednego were duly thrown into the very hot Fiery Furnace.

The King watched over these terrible proceedings with great interest. To his great surprise, and dismay he saw four figures in the furnace, he said to his servants, "Did we not cast three men into the fire?" "Yes" they replied. God had come miraculously to their rescue yet again. God was in some form with them, and protecting them from the flames.

Just a brief mention of the book called Isaiah. He was Israel's greatest Prophet. It was in 8th century BC and Isaiah prophesised in the reign of Azaria. His book, most surprisingly remained the same after many centuries, as discovered in the Great Isaiah Scroll of the Qumran community.

Turning now to the New Testament if I may, John the Baptist in the time of King Herod preached to his people the great need for repentance. He stationed himself in the wilderness by the river Jordan. He baptised those that truly repented of their sins in the river Jordon.

One day Jesus, before He started on His ministry came to John, and asked to be baptised. John was amazed, and refused Jesus's request. He told Jesus in no uncertain terms that He was not worthy to unlatch His sandals! Jesus replied that the Son of Man must be baptised, so John reluctantly obliged. There was a voice from Heaven. God said, "This is my beloved Son, in whom I am well pleased!"

King Herod put John the Baptist in prison as his wicked life contrasted sharply with John's call to repentance. He arranged a great feast for his male courtiers. In order to supply entertainment for an all-male audience he conscripted his young and beautiful daughter Salomé to entertain his guests. She readily obliged as she knew only too well how susceptible men were to female charms. She used this gift to extract the most possible out of the occasion. She appeared completely naked, and proceeded to perform a most erotic, and alluring sexual dance and display.

Herod must have thought it was his lucky day! He was so pleased that he offered to give her anything her heart desired, up to half the Kingdom. Salome retired to consider her great good fortune, and asked her mother for advice as to what she should ask for. Her mother who hated John the Baptist for his pertinent criticism of her marital status sought great revenge in telling Salome to ask for John's head on a platter. Herod was very dismayed by this totally unexpected request, as the people regarded John as a prophet. Never the less he reluctantly agreed, and John was duly decapitated, and his severed head was put on a platter and given to Salome.

Jesus set out to choose his twelve disciples. One day on the shore of Lake Galilee, He found two fisher men. They were the sons of Zebedee, James and John. Jesus said unto them, "Come and follow me." They forsook their nets, and followed Jesus.

A Jewish wedding reception was held in which Jesus, and His mother was invited. However a serious problem arose. It became apparent that the wine had run out. Mary said that Jesus was the man to help. Jesus asked for twelve large water pots to be brought, and filled to the brim with just water. Jesus then said to the servants to take them to the Master of the Feast. He tasted the miraculous water that was now wine. He called the bridegroom to point out to him that the usual custom was to provide the best wine at the beginning of the feast, followed by the least favourably variety. You he said have kept the best wine till last!

Jesus's fame quickly spread, and large crowds came to hear His message. One day on a hill in a remote area Jesus had acquired a very large audience indeed! Five thousand people had gathered to listen to His teaching. As they were not near anywhere to buy food there was a big problem. Hunger prevailed. Jesus inquired if anyone had brought any food. One boy had been sensible enough to come fully prepared. He had a basket with five barley loaves and two small fishes. Jesus asked the boy to bring the food to Him. He gave thanks as was His custom, and began to break the loaves and fishes into pieces, asking His disciples to sit the people down, and to distribute the food. Miraculously everyone had their fill, and twelve baskets of fragments of leftover food were collected at the end!

During the Roman occupation of Judea, charlatans of the Jews were recruited as tax collectors for Caesar in Rome. They were the most hated people in the land, and also very corrupt. One was a man called Zacchaeus. He was a man of short stature, so in order to see Jesus, because of the thronging crowds around Jesus; he climbed up into a sycamore fig tree.

As Jesus approached the tree He looked up and said to the amazed Zacchacous, "Come down for I want to sup with thee in thine house." The assembled onlookers were mystified as to why Jesus would want to lower Himself so much as to fraternise with a hated tax collector. Zacchaeous rose to this great occasion of entertaining Jesus in his home. He said to Jesus, "If I have defrauded anyone of any money I will repay fourfold. What a great transforming power Jesus had on people during His time on earth!

Lake Galilee was quite a large one for the area, and suffered the misfortune of unusual weather conditions. Winds without warning blew down the surrounding hillsides causing great turbulence on the surface of the water. The disciples without Jesus decided to cross the lake to reach the other side. The unexpected strong winds, which they as fishermen should have been prepared for struck with the usual ferocity. Water soon engulfed the small craft, and it began to sink. They looked around in their peril, and saw Jesus miraculously walking on the surface of the water. They naturally cried out to Him. "Carest not that we perish?" Jesus calmed the storm, and a great calm resulted! The disciples were astonished, and exclaimed, "Even the wind and waves obey Him." Over confident Peter decided to try his luck, and climbed overboard to walk like his Master on top of the water. As he took his eyes of Jesus he began to sink. He called out to Jesus to save him.

Bethany was a small place on the route to Jerusalem. Jesus had made good friends with Mary, Mather and Lazarus who lived there. On one visit Jesus was waiting for a meal which Martha was busily preparing, and as is sometimes the case she became agitated and flustered with the much work entailed in the preparation of the important meal for Jesus. Mary on the other hand had chosen wisely and was sitting next to Jesus listening intently to His word of wisdom. Mather was enraged by her sister's apparent inactivity, and said to Jesus why does not Mary help me? Jesus replied Mary has chosen the better part, and it will not be taken away from her!

The Bible records Jesus's triumphant entry into Jerusalem. He rode not on a horse as a war raging King would, but on the colt of the foal of an ass. A donkey symbolizes an animal of peace. As Jesus rode into the city He weeps over it, foretelling the suffering that awaits the city in the event of the destruction of the Second Temple. An important Jewish Holy Temple, around 516BC. It replaced Solomon's Temple which was destroyed when Jerusalem was conquered, and a portion of the population of the Kingdom of Judiah was taken into exile into Babylon.

It was customarily to cover in some way the path of someone thought worthy of a great honour. The Palm branch is a symbol of triumph and victory. The occasion is remembered today in the celebration called Palm Sunday.

The crowd as is sometimes the case were fickle, and the Chief Priests who hated Jesus for his continual criticism of their behaviour, turned the crowd against Jesus. Judas Iscariot one of the disciples betrayed his Master with a kiss. Jesus was arrested by the Priests guards, and sent for trial.

The trial was conducted by Pontius Pilate of the Roman occupation. Jesus awaiting His trial was abused by the Roman soldiers guarding Him. They clothed Him in a purple robe, and twisted a crown of thorns on His head hitting it into his skull with a stick. The Bible records that Jesus was like a lamb that is silent before the slaughter! They mocked Him by chanting, "Hail, King of the Jews!" They slapped Him on His face.

Pilate presented Jesus to His vociferous accusers, and said to them, "Here is the Man!" Jesus had already been flogged the maximum permitted of 49 lashes! The Chief Priest replied, "Crucify! Crucify!" When Pilate heard this he was even more afraid, and tried very hard to release Jesus. However the Jewish leaders knew their stuff, and taunted Pilate with these words, "If you let this man go you are no friend of Caesar!" Pilate retorted, "Here is your King!" "We have no King but

Caesar!" was the reply. Pilate surrendered ignominiously, and handed Jesus over to be crucified.

Cruelly nailed to a wooden cross, Jesus prayed to His Heavenly Father to forgive them for they know not what they do. The cruel Roman soldiers said among themselves, "Surely this was the Son of God!" Later Joseph of Arimathea who was a secret disciple of Jesus for fear of the Jews, asked Pilate for the body of Jesus. He buried the body in a stone hewn tomb with a great round stone to seal the entrance. This was in a garden.

After three days Mary Madeline a former prostitute was in the garden early in the morning. She thought that a man she approached was the Gardner. "Sir", she said, "If you have taken the body let me know so that I can care for it." She had already discovered that the huge stone at the entrance to the tomb had been rolled to one side, and to her utter amazement the tomb was empty. Jesus replied to Mary, "Mary!" She instantly recognised His voice, and went to touch His feet. Jesus rebuked her and said, "Touch me not as I have yet to ascend to my Father. Go tell my brethren".

The eleven disciples were gathered together in the Upper Room for fear of the Jews. Judas has hanged himself on a tree due to his anguish at betraying his Master for money. Jesus mysteriously appeared in the midst of them. Thomas who doubted that Jesus had risen from the dead was present. Jesus knowing all things asked Thomas to put his fingers on the nail-prints of His hands, and to trust his hand into His side to feel the wound of the spear. Jesus said to Thomas, "Be not faithless but believe!" Thomas replied, "My Lord and my God!"

The Ascension of Jesus to His Heavenly Father God in Heaven took place on the summit of the Mount of Olives. Three of His closes disciples were witnesses to this unique event. Jesus miraculously defied the law of gravity, and began to rise off the mountain top. A cloud conveniently obscured Him from view

The book of Acts written by Luke is an account of the apostle's work and life. 14 books in the New Testament have traditionally been attributed to Paul. Hebrews was not written by Paul as at first thought. Paul liked to call himself an Apostle even though he had never met Jesus on this earth. The reason he claimed this was because of his dramatic experience of conversion from Judaism to Christianity on the famous Damascus Road!

Paul, who as Saul of Tarsus changed his name on his conversion to Christianity,. He was a strict Jewish Pharisee. He was educated at the feet of the most learned teacher Gamaliel, one of the most respected Rabbis in history. Paul was the greatest and most effective missionary of the early church. He founded several churches in Asia Minor, and Europe. He was even thought to have introduced Christianity as far as Spain. As he was both a Jewish and Roman citizen he appealed to both Jewish and roman audiences.

Returning, if I may to his conversions on the Damascus road. He had authority from the Chief priests to bring those Christians that he found in Damascus bound to Jerusalem for summary punishment.

However never remotely in his mind, something life changing happened. There was a great light, and a voice from Heaven which said to him, "Paul, why persecutes thou me?!" Those with Paul thought that it thundered.

Paul was temporally blinded, and lost his sight for three days. He was led into Damascus where a most surprised and wary Ananias a Christian who Paul came to take prisoner, prayed with Paul, and his sight was restored.

Paul liked to refer to himself as being of the stock or Israel, of the tribe of Benjamin, a Hebrew of the Hebrews, as touching the law a Pharisee!

All seemed to go well for Paul for a long time. His style of preaching was notably successful. However there was one fly in the ointment as he fell out with Barnabus a missionary colleague. Paul's run of good luck eventually came to an end. There was a lot of very powerful opposition to his new teaching. He found himself put into prison in chains! One day King Agrippa 11, a great grandson Herod the Great, who attempted to kill the infant Jesus, and who did kill many young boys in Judea.

King Agrippa's father, king Agrippa 1 beheaded the apostle James, and arrested

Peter in an attempt to kill him. King Agrippa 11 did not have any children when he met Paul, and was in an incestuous relationship with his sister Queen Bernice. He was a pervert who lived with many different people. His capital was Caesarea Philippi. He was very friendly with Caesar.

Paul predicament came to King Agrippa's attention, and partly for entertainment and curiosity he summoned Paul before him to give his defence for what he believed was his unjust detention. Paul gave a summary of his life and Christian ministry. He told the King confidently that he genuinely wished him to be the same as himself except for my chains. Festive the Governor was also present, and he interjected rudely to say, "Paul thy much learning hast made thee mad!"

Paul realised that the game was up, and that he was getting no further on here, so as a Roman citizen he used his right to appeal to Caesar in Rome. This entailed a long and in those days perilous journey. On arrival in Rome he was greeted by the newly converted Christians, but he was however put under house arrest. This lasted for many long years.

The Acts of Paul, an apocryphal work around 160 AD describes the martyrdom of Paul. Nero condemned Paul to death by decapitation. This happened around the time of the fire of Rome 64 AD.

Returning to Paul's much writings which form much of present day theology, includes what he calls the essence of the Christian Message.

1 – God sent His Son.

2 – The Son was crucified for the sins of humanity.

3 – After being dead for three days the Son was raised from the dead, defeating death.

4 – The Son would soon return. (Which He obviously has not!)

5 – Those in Christ will live with Him for ever.

6 – Followers are urged to live by a set apart.

I pray God your whole spirit and soul and body will be presented blameless unto the coming of our Lord Jesus Christ.

Paul was convinced that Jesus would return in his lifetime. I wonder how it would have affected his belief if he knew that his Lord had not returned for over 2000 years!

Paul said in his letter to the Galatian church, "There is neither Jew nor Gentile, neither slave or free, nor is there male or female, for you are all one in Christ Jesus.

Paul's views about women were however rather jaundiced. He said not to suffer a woman to teach, and to learn in silence with sobriety. This has led throughout history to the subordination of woman, and is the reason why men are always considered the head of the household! Brilliant woman authors had to publish under a male pseudonym, otherwise they would be thought as not serious writers.

I propose to end this journey through Holy Scripture with a candid appraisal of the last book in the Bible written by John the disciple whom Jesus loved the book of Revelation. In my considered view the language is very colourful and almost psychedelic. Google puts it this way, Revelation is extravagant imagery!

Martin Luther called it neither apostolic nor prophetic. It was the only book in the whole Bible that John Calvin did not write a commentary on! In D. H. Lawrence's Apocalypse he said the language used in the book of Revelation was bleak and destructive, a 'Death Product!' The wrath of the Lamb was ridiculous!

Some of the imagery and language used in this book is very disturbing indeed! 'And to them it was given that they should not kill them but that they should be tormented for five months, and their torment was as the torment of a scorpion when it striketh man! And in those days men shall seek death and shall not find it, and death shall flee from them.

There will be terrible punishment and retribution for those, nearly all today, who engage in sexual activity outside of marriage. Also the same fate for prostitutes, even though Jesus was related to Rehab the Harlot a prostitute!

In closing my I remark to my readers that in my view there is a very great dichotomy ever present in the Bible. Principally, the conflict between one view of God as a loving and benevolent

Father figure, and the great paradox of a megalomaniacal, tyrannical sadist.

I hope very much that whatever you think that I will have brought some stimulus to the ever ongoing debate of religion!

Many sincere thanks and goodbye.

IS RELIGIOUS BELIEF REALLY NECESSARY?

The short answer is NO! Please let me quickly reassure my readers that I believe that we should be free to believe what we choose. I believe strongly in religious freedom as so many terrible crimes in history have been committed against people when this was not allowed. I believe that religious belief has caused many more problems than it has solved.

There is a positive, and I am sorry to say, also a negative side to it as well. Believers naturally promote the positive side. That God is a God of great love, compassion, and forgiveness, slow to anger, and plenteous in mercy. The legacy of this is the most beautiful architecture, music, poetry, and not forgetting good works!

The negative side, never mentioned by believers, is the most appalling, and horrific crimes against humanity throughout history. I believe we should all try to learn from our history.

What I understand about religious belief is taken from my knowledge of the Bible, although I have not read from it since I was a child! I do seem to have an incredible memory. I have though considered the issues all my life of 73 years. I have a very logical mind.

The Bible is made up of many separate books and writers. I believe that the Bible message is to try to give a plausible explanation for the existence of good and evil, and the necessary salvation offered by God for sin. The Bible states "How shall we escape if we neglect so great a salvation!"

I believe that the vast mass of the universe is far beyond all human understanding. That it is far too big for any human concept of a god-like figure to create from nothing. It is not a sensible or rational belief. The 'Big Bang' theory which says that there is an endless expansion, and contraction of the universe. This is followed, because of the force of gravity which is so very great on very large masses in the universe with a contraction eventually into a single mass, and because of its great density it explodes again, and so it is repeated for ever more. At the moment scientists believe that our universe is in the expanding mode. Believers say that the universe is a powerful indication that a god- like figure must have been responsible for it. This beggars all belief!

Galileo believed that the earth went around the sun. He was threatened with prison and worse by the religious leaders of his day who believed that the sun went around the earth which observing the sun it seems to do. Everyone now believes that Galileo was correct and the church was terribly wrong in believing they were infallible.

The roman emperor Constantine decided which books to include and which to leave out. This Holy Book has remained more or less the same since then. I believe that Constantine embraced this religion and made it the state religion. The Bible claims that Almighty God inspired the writers with his message to all mankind for all time.

You may find it strange that I love the Bible, particularly the King James Version. The language is so grand, authoritative, and beautiful. Modern translations do not compare at all, although they may be a little more accurate. It was very easy for the Bible writers to accept miracles and a belief in the supernatural, which with scientific knowledge is much more difficult for us today. I love the stories in the Bible.

I think some of them are the best ever written. They are short and very concise. I try to copy this style in my writing. At boarding school I was hopeless at English, but I was good at précis.

Andrew Lloyd-Webber who knows a good story when he sees one chose the Bible story of Joseph in the Old Testament, for his hit musical, 'Joseph and the Multi-Coloured Dream Coat.' This was a drama about hatred, suffering, reconciliation, and forgiveness. Other favourites are Jesus's great story about what it is to be a good neighbour. 'The Good Samaritan'. He was the most unlikely man in the whole world to help the injured Jew. The Jews and the Samaritans had no dealings with each other. The Chief Priest who was the most likely man on the scene to help passed by on the other side of the road. Jesus was always very critical of the religious leaders of His day. One day they had confronted a woman taken in adultery. They asked Jesus if they should stone her to death, which was the Jewish law of the day. Jesus replied, "He that is without sin may cast the first stone." Jesus said to the woman," Does no one condemn you? Go sin no more." Jesus was once invited to the home of Judas. He insulted Jesus by not washing his feet which was the usual custom. Mary Madeleine a prostitute put things right by washing Jesus's feet with her tears, and drying them with her hair. She anointed his feet with very expensive ointment. Judas Iscariot a disciple of Jesus who kept their purse and stole from it said, "Should not this ointment been sold for 200 pence and given to the poor?" Jesus replied, "She who is forgiven much loveth much. Jesus, to me, is an extremely attractive character indeed. Better than His Heavenly Father God. His teaching on morality known as the Sermon on the Mount, it is exemplary, and has never been equalled.

God the Father is understandably thought of as a God of great love, as he sent His perfect Son to redeem the world, by being cruelly put to death on the cross so we could be united with Him in all eternity, and escape God's terrible punishment for sin.

I wish to point out from the Bible some stories which do not seem to agree with this view. In the Old Testament during the time of a man known as Noah. God found that mankind was so wicked that He decided to kill all living things which He had created except Noah and all his family in a worldwide flood. I ask what did all the children, babies, and the animals do wrong? It is very unlikely that all men and woman were wicked. Later the Bible recorded that God repented of what He had done, and put the rainbow in the sky as a sign that He would never destroy mankind again. God's act of seeming savage genocide has never been equalled by evil men! Almighty God should be held to account for this greatest crime in all history. It is surely a paradox that He is said to find evil abhorrent! The spectacle of Almighty, all knowing God admitting to a great mistake is extremely puzzling indeed. To my mind it puts into question all God's alleged attributes!

As I expect you may have guessed that I am an atheist. I understand that this belief will offend some believers. Unlike some believers, I do not hate, injure or kill anyone, like the present day Islamic State, which threatens to kill all those who do not share their beliefs.

My long considered view is that Almighty God is in fact just a human creation, and that He does not exist in reality. It has been a very long gestation period indeed! My belief is strengthened by the Bible story of the ancient Jews who were called Israelites at that time of their journey into the promised land of Canaan. God said He would give this land to them, and that it was a land of 'Milk and Honey'. What a description! They found that the Canaanites made their gods out of wood and stone. Although they believed their creation were real gods, who would help them, like believers today think of their God. The ancient Jews did not think they were real gods, so they made a great step forward in theology by creating their God with their minds! The great advantage of this was that their God could not be scrutinised, like the gods of wood and stone. This view of God by more than one religion has stood the test of time. It is safely beyond the scrutiny of modern science. This is why it prevails.

Turning once again to my conviction that religious belief is not essential to a fulfilled and happy life, and that it has far more problems with it than it solves, I mentioned at the beginning the advantages on the positive side, now I want to discuss the more negative aspects of religious belief. It causes people to hate each other, strife, and intolerance even death and genocide. I will give you a few examples from history and modern times. The religious crusades to the Holy Land in the Middle East in the Middle Ages. and the savage destruction of the Inca civilisation by the Spanish in South America, the burning at the stake of a man called William Tyndyle. He fell out with the religious powers of his day for translating the Bible into English. Arch Bishop Thomas Cranmer held a different interpretation on religion than the people in power. He was made to recant in prison, but later he changed his mind, and was then burnt at the stake. He said that he would put his hand into the flames around him first! What a great and very brave man indeed. The vast country of India had to be partitioned because two different religions wanted to kill each other. Ghandi pleaded with both sides to show tolerance and respect, but they refused to listen to their revered leader, even when he went on hunger strike to try and solve the fighting between two different religions, but they refused to listen. That is why we now have India and Pakistan. The hatred killings and trouble for 30 years in Northern Ireland between rival religious beliefs.

This is why I believe the negative side out ways the positive side decisively. With the rise of Islamic State often in the news today because of the awful atrocities they commit. The suicide bombers believe they will go to a much better eternity if they die as martyrs. They do it in the name of the same God of other religions! In the long run while I believe in religious freedom, this may have to be discouraged just in order for us all to survive, and to protect our way of life and the principles we live by. People all around the world, are beginning to wonder if religious belief is really such a good idea after all. We are always told just how good it is. Blindness seems to be an essential part of religious belief!

The fundamental stories in the Bible which support a belief in God are The Virgin Birth, the Resurrection, and the Ascension. They have never been able to be scrutinised by science. Then we have the story in the book of Revelation of the graves being opened, and the sea giving up its dead followed by the final Judgment, to sort out the sheep from the goats! These fanciful stories which are so far-fetched make it very difficult to understand why anyone would believe them. Particularly, educated leaders of religious belief.

Just a brief mention of one difficulty, what happens to the many people who have been cremated? How is their body put together again?

After Jesus was raised from the dead He appeared in the midst of the upper room where the eleven Disciples were meeting. Why there was not twelve was because Judas Iscariot had hanged himself on a tree, because of his remorse at betraying Jesus his master for money. Jesus asked Thomas who doubted that Jesus had risen from the dead, to put his hand on the nail-prints on his hands, and thrust his hand into the spear wound on His side. Jesus told 'Doubting -Thomas', "Be not faithless but believe." He replied, "My Lord and my God!" Just as a little aside, faith can never prove anything, but it can allow you to believe in anything you like. This is how religious believers cope with the anomalies of their conviction. In my life I have decided to try to stand up for what is right, and what can be proved to be true, not a belief in incredible fables!

Just to return to the above, Jesus's 'risen' body that would shortly travel all the way to Heaven, was strangely not perfect. Thomas saw for himself that Jesus's body had the hall-marks of His cruel death on the cross. I wonder what peoples 'risen' body will be like if they have lost limbs or are deformed. There will never be an answer probably.

*****

May I pause here to share a little of my background with my readers. My parents were strict non-conformist evangelical religious believers. I was instructed in their belief from my birth. I was made to kneel down at my bed and say my prayers to God out loud for my mother to hear. At the tender age of 11 years I was sent 250 miles away to a co-educational boarding school. I had never been there before. I found myself in a dormitory of 40 boys. My mother unwisely had made me promise to kneel down and continue to say my prayers. I looked around to see if any of the other boys did the same. No one did, so I was too afraid to. I went to sleep sobbing as I had broken my promise to my dear mother.

*****

*****

I was a complete and utter failure at school. I left at the age of 15 with only 20% in English Language. I could not write or spell very well but I could always read. I went home to manage my parent's dairy farm as my father was unwell. I enjoyed this for six years when it was sold so my parents could retire. I then spent my working life as a Laboratory Technician in several different schools. I never had a professional job. I know a lot about depression, suffering, and despair for many years of my life. Just recently I have discovered that I can write after all! When I was only 12 years old, in church, I came to the conclusion, completely on my own, that it did not make any sense at all for a loving God to send the vast majority of mankind to Hell to be punished for not believing in His Son Jesus's salvation plan for all humanity. I even went against my dear parent's belief. The religious belief that I had been indoctrinated in from birth, I felt it was now not true. I never confided this to my dear mother all her life as it would have hurt her terribly.

My ex-wife and I had to go to Family Courts for the custody of my son. I won but was granted very limited access to Samuel My interests are as follows- I am a very keen photographer. The walls of my lounge at my home in Cullompton, Devon, are completely covered with my A4 colour photographs. The Queen has seen some of them, and has told me that they were splendid! I love music that is beautiful to hear. This is mainly Classical but some of the best Popular and Country Music as well. Patsy Cline, 'If I could only see the world through the eyes of a child, what a wonderful world it would be – A Blue Bird in every tree'! Jim Reeves, Four Walls. Music is so therapeutic. I am an excellent chef, and love to entertain guests to dinner, but I never bother to cook for myself! I have found great happiness late in my life, through meeting and getting to know as many people on my many walks around town as possible each day. I even talk to strangers who always seem to feel better for speaking to me. I find it extremely rewarding. I recommend it! I believe that being friendly, courteous and polite is very infectious indeed. It spreads. That is why my home town of Cullompton in Devon is so very friendly!

I wish to say a big thank you to all the people who have helped me, and made it possible for me to be able to write my book. The Librarians at the Hayridge Library, in particular with her help with troublesome computers, and Justine Lopez my Publishing Consultant in America for her unwavering encouragement, even as a believer, to write my book, and not forgetting my very best friend Graham Slade my friend for 40 years who gave me great support and encouragement. Thanks to who have kept me mentally well so I could write such an important book.

To return to my case, let us consider the first book in the Bible called Genesis. It is always a good thing to start at the beginning. I believe it was written by Moses the leader of the Israelites from their slavery in Egypt to the promised land of Canaan. On the first page is the story of God's creation of all things in the universe. This story is now often an embarrassment to believers, as it clearly states that God created it all in six days, and on the seventh day He rested. I should think so! Apologists sometimes try to claim that it was not a 'day' of 24 hours, they overlook that it says very clearly 'The morning and evening of each day. Even more embarrassing is in the second book of the Bible, Exodus chapter 20, in the ten commandment given to Moses by God on a mountain top for his chosen people, one of them is 'Remember the Sabbath Day to keep it Holy', and to do no work, as the Lord thy God rested on the seventh day after all His work with creation. Most rational people and modern day science believe that creation took millions of years, with living things evolving very slowly from the simple to the most complex forms of life. Charles Darwin's theory of evolution in his classic book 'The Origin of the Species ', gave a modern and acceptable explanation for scientists, although it is still only a theory. It is, however much more plausible than the six days by God. Perhaps the real answer is that we may never know!

As we travel through the Bible we come to the New Testament written in Greek. The Old Testament is written in the Hebrew language. The first four books are

Mathew, Mark, Luke, and John. They were disciples of Jesus. They all write a detailed account of Jesus's life here on earth. The problem is that it is believed they were not written until about a hundred years after Jesus's crucifixion and death. They most probably were dead by then. In any case it was a very long time to remember such detail.

The last book in the Bible is Revelations. This is a colourful and almost psychedelic writing. It tells us about the end of the world, God's final Judgement of mankind, and who will go to Heaven, and who will be sent to Hell for eternity. Hell is a very interesting concept indeed. It is the place, not specified where it actually is, where the Devil, originally a very important angel in heaven long before creation of mankind, dwells with his angels. It is a place of terrible suffering and torment. The Bible says the Devil will be put by God into a bottomless pit. There is to be a Lake of Fire. The idea of everlasting punishment by a loving God is very difficult for believers to come to terms with. Hell features in more than one religion. They pick and choose what to believe in the Bible. There is never any consensus about which parts of the Bible to believe or not to believe. Lastly may I mention to my readers that Revelations has the story of Jesus's 'Second Coming'. He will appear in the sky, and it says that every eye will see Him, TV? Unlike His previous appearance on earth, He will return in power and glory, triumphant even over death itself. 'Death where is thy victory!'? He will rule the world for a 1000 years! God's Judgement will follow, and only those who names are written in the 'Lamb's Book of Life' because they have believed in Jesus and His offer of salvation, will be accepted in Heaven for ever more. The rest of humanity will be sent to Hell for eternity to suffer for evermore. There is no 'middle ground' offered in the Bible. This is very clear in the Bible message.

The early church believed that Jesus would return very soon. He said that He was going to prepare a place in Heaven. "Know ye not that there are many mansions in my Father's house!" The early church would have been shocked to the very core if they knew Jesus had not returned for over 2000 years. Maybe, it is just because He is no longer alive.

There is an often repeated old argument that parts of the Bible are not meant to be taken literally. The problem for me is, who is going to decide which bits of the Bible are literal, and which are not. There is never any agreement on this by believers. My dear mother said that if you can't believe some of it why believe any of it. This is a logical argument. Also it is unlikely that God would have made it complicated, as it was His most important message to all mankind for all time. It should be taken at face value I believe. A few years ago Channel 4 TV had a two hour program called Is religion the root of all evil?! It was very convincing. It may not be the root of all evil, but is certainly some of it!

In the Bible God said that homosexuality was an abomination to Him. This has led to the terrible persecution of this most unfortunate minority throughout history. We now know that it is a condition you are born with and people cannot help. The cruel destruction by God of the cities of Sodom and Gomorrah with fire and brimstone because of their homosexuality. Righteous Lot and his wife were saved however, but as they fled his wife looked back at the city, and was turned into a pillar of salt for her pains. This is good illustration of the benefits of the scientific method of inquiry is to us all. It is so much better than bigoted and unproven demands of Holy Scripture! The reason why I so prefer the verdicts of scientific inquiry is the reason for the great and many successes of science, like landing a man on the moon, or all the great benefits of the many vaccinations available

IS RELIGIOUS BELIEF REALLY NECESSARY?

today, or the tremendous convenience of mobile phones. Nearly everyone the world today has one. I have recently purchased one with a FM radio, and powerful torch for just £5! The many great successes of science for more examples like computers, the internet, Skype, all free to all in our world. In mentioning vaccinations, which prevent even killer diseases. The famous scientist Jenner noticed that girls who milked cows contracted cowpox, but they never got the deadly killer smallpox. Science is about making very correct observations about our world. Jenner had the first brilliant idea of making a vaccine from cowpox. Smallpox was quickly banished. Antibiotics are another great triumph for science. Again if science was not true they would not work at all. Religious believers have in the main a jaundice view of science, as that is what is defeating some of their many bizarre beliefs or religion! I readily understand that at the moment science cannot fully explain how the creation of the universe came about, and therefore why many people believe that there must have been a god-like figure behind it. The fact that we cannot understand it is not a good reason to embrace a totally unbelievable power of a god, who can create from nothing the unimaginable mass and energy of the universe. It simply just does not make any sense at all. I feel it is, with our present knowledge that it is not rational or logical.

Changing the subject a little, hardly anyone chooses to get married in church with God's blessing. The vows you have to make which are beautifully concise and are very optimistic indeed. Most people decide they are too unrealistic to keep to.

Religious believers have an old and often used argument to get themselves, out of a tight corner. They claim and believe in 'The Spiritual Realm.' An example of this is Jesus's ascension to Heaven, our 'risen' bodies, and Heaven and Hell themselves. My answer to this is, that this allows anyone to add anything they like to the 'Spiritual Realm', which they cannot explain in any other way, and cannot be proved. I cannot accept this dodging of the issue by believers.

Why throughout early history mankind has always had a belief in a god albeit a very vague one. This is due to the precarious nature of early civilisations.

Illness, disease, and even death were rife. This encouraged a belief in the supernatural who they also believed would give them victory in battle. All people in history have had a great difficulty in coming to terms with their mortality.

In Russia the communist's in power tried to suppress a belief in God. It was because they felt that this made it more possible for the proletariat to accept poorer conditions in life, because the church made them believe that it did not matter too much, as eternity would at last be so very wonderful. I feel that to recognise this is the only existence we have focus's the mind on making the fullest use of our present life. I have tried very hard not to be offensive to anyone of good will. I accept that their beliefs are sincere.

Although I am not a believer I find religion an extremely interesting subject which stimulates the mind and intellect. As a source of truth which I find essential, science has a much greater track record than religious belief. Science has rarely got it wrong like religion has done so many times in all our history!

It would seem from reading the Bible that rebellion and evil, which I believe in, came directly from within Heaven itself, long before the creation of Adam and Eve. The Bible records that Lucifer, the Devil, fell like the morning star. What another brilliant description? The Devil was allowed by God to wreck His perfect creation single-handedly! The devil in the guise of a Serpent tempted Adam and Eve to eat of the forbidden fruit, gaining the knowledge of good and evil. This led to the 'Fall', and the imperfect world we all have to live in. The Devil was a very important Angel in God's household. If God had not lost control in Heaven then there would have been no rebellion, and no one to lead Adam and Eve astray. The perfect creation may have remained. We read that God communed with them in the cool of the day. There would have been no need for the 'Judgement' or terrible Hell. At the end of God's creation He said that it was good, after each day of His work of creating.

Is it possible that God needed the Devil to test Adam and Eve? The tremendous cost of this 'luxury' lay at the feet of the whole human race, and in the crucifixion and death of God's perfect Son. In theology the 'Trinity' explains that Jesus was God and also the Holy Spirit. I believe that it was far too costly to have been the case. God has knowledge of all things past, present and in the future.

At the end of the world, and judgment, could there be during eternity a repeat of one or more important angels rebelling against God again? After all, God had this trouble before, and He seems to be not all powerful. The human race has had to pay the terrible price for God's lack of control. The terrible, unlimited, and eternal punishment in Hell, with the Devil and his angels, is surely out of all proportion to the alleged offence. Compassion, God's alleged attribute seems to be completely lacking!

If God is as the Bible says is all powerful, all knowing, and hates sin, how is it that He did not foresee the rebellion in Heaven. Why did He knowingly let one of His important angels wreck His perfect creation of man created in God's own image for companionship for Himself. Can God be really trusted with our eternal future at all?

In summary this is the reason why as a child of 12 years old I came to the rational and logical conclusion, that the story outlined in the Bible, was therefore untrue. Turning to the question of 'freewill'. Is there to be free will in eternity in Heaven? If the answer is YES then there can be future rebellions. If NO, and God is happy with this, then why have free will in the first place? If there is to be NO free will, then God's creation would have remained perfect! Surely this is far more preferable to all the evil, sin, and human suffering since the 'fall' at the very beginning of history, which will be with us throughout eternity in Hell!

If we accept that God hates sin and evil, the perfect creation with Adam and Eve communing with God their creator in the cool of the day, as the Bible so wonderfully puts it, is surely preferable to all the sin, evil, and human suffering throughout history. Also the cruel death on the cross of His perfect Son God incarnate in human flesh. Let us not forget all those whose names are not written in the 'Lamb's Book of Life'. Their lot will be torment and terrible suffering in Hell for eternity, or if you like, for ever more! Jesus's death on the cross will never end human suffering in Hell which there is no end. God's salvation plan seems not to perfect. My conclusion is, if we accept that religious belief is NOT a certainty if it requires faith, then everything I have claimed and said falls neatly into place.

We have now come to the end of a long journey and you may be saying to me that I may have a point of view, but we are at a great loss to know what would replace all our time, energy, and resources we have devoted to our religious belief. May I appeal to the great majority of people of good will in our world, and say to them that I have the perfect answer.

Let me say is there not a great deal of good works waiting to be done in our world today. There is poverty, injustice, bigotry, intolerance, sickness, and loneliness. Need I go on? Let us together try to give up what is divisive, intolerant, strife, mistrust, and I am afraid to say hatred.

What a great vision this would be for our beloved children, and all future generations to come. May I end this main part of my book to thank most sincerely all my readers who have waded this far through my first ever book!

CLASSICAL MUSIC ACCORDING TO MAURICE!

I believe the very pinnacle of Classical Music belongs, quite rightly to the greatest genius ever to have lived in our world, Wolfgang Amadeus Mozart. He lived among us some 200 years ago. His homeland was Austria, and he resided in the city of Saltsburg. His native language was German.

He was a child prodigy and his father Leopold Mozart also a composer, took advantage of his brilliant son's amazing abilities, and brought him to London to give piano recitals. At the infant age of six he stunned everyone around him by composing his first symphony. It did not stop there; at the age of twelve he composed his first opera in the Italian language, as was the custom for operas because of the language's beautiful sound for the human voice. What a notable and absolutely stunning achievement?!

Mozart's private life was however often strained. His marriage to his wife Costanzia was not an easy one. Tragedy struck very early in his very short life. His wife died of consumption, and also his young children died. Mozart died penniless, and had to be buried outside the city in a proper's grave.

Mozart was a very busy and productive composer indeed! Over 40 symphonies are to his credit. Over 20 piano concertos, as well as a great number of concertos for individual instruments, of which Mozart excelled in playing himself! The clarinet, flute, flute and harp, and horn come to my mind. There were also many most beautify piano sonatas. His choral work, Lachrymose is a real delight. Also the Turkish March.

My task in this book of mine is to bring to your attention, and hopefully your agreement, some of his greatest compositions.

Possibly as a strong contender for the top position would be his clarinet concerto, followed by his piano concerto number 21. His concertos for the horn are also very popular! His concerto for flute and harp is absolutely delightful! Some other composers have some compositions which I do not care very much for, but it is very difficult to find just one that would not give you spell-binding pleasure!

The obvious question is who would follow next after this enviable position? The answer is not too difficult. I suggest to you Ludwig Von Beethoven. A German, who knew Mozart and was a friend of his, maybe there were not so many, and so varied compositions as Mozart, but his nine symphonies are considered to be on a very grand and triumphant scale!

Beethoven, like Mozart, had his share of great problems. He became completely deaf at the very young age of 26! However, the great man continued to compose great music, without being able to hear it! Is this not incredible?!

My very favourite piano concerto is his number five known as the Emperor. Also I particularly find it mentally very satisfying his piano sonata number 40, The Moon Light. When I was a small child at school I tried to play his Fleur Elise on the piano. This was possible, as very unusually in Classical Music it had no sharps or flats! The piano piece known as The Pathetique, and the orchestral arrangement of Beethoven's Romance No. 02 is also very good on the human ear. In passing his sonata 'al Chiaro di Lina, is well worth a mention.

Just today on YOU TUBE UK there to be hidden away is the most sublime piano sonata – Silencio – silence! In addition, if this was not enough there is hidden away on YOU TUBE, Beethoven's – Historia de Amor! Beethoven's piano sonatas, a catalogue of them all, played one after the other on YOU TUBE, with no annoying adverts has attracted 15 million viewers! I was surprised to find on YOU TUBE a Sinfonia 'Titanic', as in the film score!

Beethoven was not always a very agreeable man, and often complained about service at restaurants. His ill humour may have been due to the very great aggravation at the loss of his hearing.

Let us now turn to a composer with English connections John Field. He was an

Irishman who emigrated the short distance to England in the 1700's. He quickly established himself as an impressive pianist. He did not rest on his laurels, and was a prolific composer. Notably for his favourite instrument the piano. He is credited with the invention of the Nocturne. A gentle and peaceful piece for his beloved piano, very suitable for night-time listening.

This leads me nicely on to Frederick Francois Chopin. He is Poland's most famous son. However, best known to himself he left his homeland for Paris where he then decided to stay and compose his memorable and very brilliant music. He composed many pieces for the piano, but only two piano concertos. The Minuet Waltz, Les Elf ide, and The Spring waltz are firm favourite, and Tristesse. His Mazurkes, one known as Marinarel'a, will not disappoint!

He had a friendship with Franz Liszt, and was greatly admired by Robert Schumann. In 1835 he obtained French citizenship, and died in Paris in 1849, age 39, properly of tuberculosis. He was very young to die like Mozart. His compositions were influenced by polish folk music, and in the classical tradition of Mozart and Schubert.

He composed many Nocturnes like John Field did, and it is sometimes wrongly thought that Chopin was the founder of the Nocturne.

I must pause here; I have made a very recent discovery. Julius Fucik. He was a

Czech of fairly recent times. He is credited with composing over 200 pieces of music. These beautiful and instantly memorable pieces include many waltzes and marches. They compare very well with the prolific waltz kings the Strass family. The marches compare with the famous American Liberty Bell march by John Philip Sousa.

Here is a short list of my favourites.

1 – The Thunder and Blazes March.

2 – Entry of the Gladiators. Often played and well known at Circus's.

3 – Florentine Marsch, played by a percussion ensemble, as is most of his music. There are no violins!

4 – Marinarella, a piece just for the piano.

5 – Ballerinas Waltz, Op, 226.

6 – Osterreichischer Militarmarsch, 'Die Regimentskinder.

7 – Merry Country Blacksmith.

8 – Wiener Phillarmoniker – Stary brucoun humorska.

9 – Osterreichischer Militamarsch, die Regimentskinder.

10 – His version of The beautiful blue Danue.

In my list of the top three composers Tchaikovsky is widely included in a list of the top three. He was thought to be a homosexual, and when this was found out he decided to kill himself. How very sad?!

His legacy was his very well-known overture 1812. The Nutcracker – The Sugar Plum fairy, and the Italian Symphony. March slave. Waltz, of the Flowers. The ballet Swan Lake.

Another Russian that comes to my mind is Dimitri Shostakovich. He was well liked by the Communists that were in power, and Joseph Stain awarded him Russia greatest honour The Order of Lenin. Many people know and love his film score to the film The Gad Fly. It is called Romance. He is the only composer that I know that has combined the classical music tradition with a very strange bedfellow indeed. The rhythms of Jazz music. This is expertly achieved in his Jazz Suit 1 and 2. His piano concerto No. 2 is well loved. His son has followed in his father's footsteps.

Now I must tell my readers that my favourite instrument out of so very many good choices, we are always spoilt for choice with classical music, is the Spanish Classical Guitar. Two pieces for this instrument, and I forgot to mention why I liked it so very much was because of the great simplicity of the sound it produces coupled with and the extraordinary delightful sound. To return if I may to these two pieces which almost anyone interested in serious music can recognise the melody if not the name are, Anonymous Air – Traditional, and Memories of the Alhambra. Albinoni with his Adagio in G Minor has a well-deserved place here.

A really energetic and vibrant piece for the guitar is Paco De Lucia – Tico Tico. If you have never heard this amazing music, I suggest to you that you have never lived. House-wives if you bogged down with the necessary ironing, and all the chores, switch on and have a fling around the kitchen! Also listen to Paco – Entre dos aguas, Great music!

While digressing for a short while on music with an infectious beat and rhythm, which causes us all of every age to drop everything and dance the night away. It's very puzzling indeed why all the greatest composers mostly never wrote, or discovered this kind of music.

On YOU TUBE UK, there is more music than I had ever in my wildest dreams believed ever existed. The free choice there is phenomenal with the greatest range, and to suit all tastes. While I accept that the concert hall is a great real-life experience that will always be popular. However having the great convinces of your own instant choice, and the very great experience of all kinds of music that you did not know existed.

Let me make some suggestions from my own personal and very recent discoveries. Jerome Robert.

1 – Adios Amor Adios.

2 – La valse d'lnnsbruck, complete with the amazing playing of very tiny cow bells!

3 – L'arc en ciel tyrolien.

4 – Bell Tyrolienne.

5 – Belle tyrdienne.

6 – La valse des anous.

7 – La valse d'lnnsbruck.

8 – Larc en ciel tyrolien.

Patrick Sebastien.

1 – CA CA song.

Demise Roussos a famous Greek singer of some age now, and quite portly, has a great number of the most heart-warming songs every written! He has in many people's opinion a most wonderful and amazing tenor voice. May I suggest that you just click on YOU TUBE and Demise and indulge in a musical feast of delight! What about, 'Una Plamo Blanka? 'No one can take my freedom away'! The sun shines on the mountains. I am just a bird in the sky. I can feel the morning sunlight, and smell the new mown hay!

This song is featured by more than just won artist.

Una Paloma blanca – Commentca va par L'Orchestre de Christophe Demerson. This version is guaranteed to take your breath away!

I never realised that so much music was suited to the Accordion. Just tap Accordion music into YOU TUBE, and you will be amazed!

Having strayed of course somewhat let us return to more academic pursuits!

Maurice Ravel, my Christian name! Bolero. This music is rather unique in its construction starting of very quietly with a short continually repeated tune gradually increasing in volume until reaching a crescendo finally at the end.

Camille Saint-Saens is most widely remembered for The Swan. This is part of several pieces in The Carnival of the Animals. The Swan is correctly depicted paddling effortlessly on the river in great grace and serenity! Also to recommend is The Aquarium. He also composed a very great work called his Organ Symphony, No 3.

Let us turn our attention to British composers. Sir Edward Elgar. Properly, best remembered for The Pomp and

Circumstance No. 1, and the very famous and well-known cello concerto. This has never been performed better than in the classic interpretation by Jacqueline du Prey. Her brilliant musical career came to an abrupt and very cruel end with the illness Muscular Dystrophy. She was married to a present-day brilliant musician Daniel Barenboim. Let us not forget Elgar's 'Serenade.'

Coming right up to date, a present-day composer, very well received by the general public, is Sir Karl Jenkins. His work known as The Armed Man is always being requested, particularly the part called Benedictus!

Another well-known artist from Wales is Kathleen Jenkins. Not only a great interpreter of opera, but also a most delightfully modest, heart-warming, and homely, young lady. She is also blessed with wonderful appearance and good-looks!

Carl von Webber's Jubilee Overture solves the perennial problem of where the tune of our National Anthem comes from. Puzzles no more! It is the last part of this Overture!

Returning if I may to Germany, the birth-place and home of so many of the very greatest of all composers is Franz Schubert. I very much appreciate his sixth symphony, and his Quintet 'The Trout.' His piece for two piano's and four pairs of hands is The March Militia! Let us not forget his Serenade and Impromptu, and a most memorable work 'Ave Maria,' and his German Mass the Sanctus.

Johann Sebastian Back, 1685 – 1750. There were three brothers, called Carl Phillipp Emanuel Bach, and Johann Christian Bach, all notable composers in their own right. He was, like so many of the world's greatest composers German, of the Barque period.

Famous music-maker Andre Rieu on recounting his life-long passion for the most beautiful and sublime music said of Bach, that his music infused goodness and love! He had a Stradivarius violin that he astonished people by saying that the world's greatest constructor of violins, that the wood he constructed them from had to be dried for 100 years! As a young child Andre Rieu would retire to his small bedroom and practice his violin and his scales, which he still has to do even today! He said, like Martin Luther King, that he was a dreamer! His story is brought to us on YOU TUBE where the compiled musical compositions are called 'Love Songs!

Andre Rieu explained to us that his most successful career as a musician and conductor gave him the very greatest pleasure possible! That music, called once is the food of love! It was very beneficial and promoted good health! He backed this with a very proud bost, that during the last 30 years, he and all his very large orchestra, had never had even one day's illness!

He went on to recall that he started out giving his unique style of concerts, which have become such a very great success all over the world, with just five musicians and only two very small cars for transport between concert venues. Now he said he travels all over the world giving his concerts to thousands of delighted audiences, not in two small cars, but in a massive jet! He said that he, and his very large orchestra, with other performers travels in great style in a huge jet, to every continent in the world, for many weeks at a time, they are never home-sick, as they get so much pleasure through just being able to enthral, and delight audiences as no other world class orchestra has ever achieved before.

We have already mentioned Franz Liszt, so here are some of my favourites – Liebestraum – Love Dream No.

3. He composed many pieces for the piano on which he was a very proficient performer.

Antonin Dvorak – New World Symphony, is well-known as it was used in the long-running advert for Hovis bread!

Bedrich Smetana – 1824 – 1884 well-loved work is Ma Vlast Moldau.

Pachelbel – Canon in D Minor is well-known.

George Frederick Handle is understandably regarded as British as he lived here in London, where you can still visit his house. However he was born in Germany. As well as a very great composer he was an accomplished organist, and composed an organ symphony. Other works are the great choral work The Messiah.

The Royal Fireworks. Handel's Largo, the Sarbanes.

Catachurian – The Ballet 'Spartacus and Fridgea.' This was featured in the BBC TV series 'The Onedian Line.'

Giuseppe Fortuncio Francesco Verdi, an Italian from a provincial family of moderate means. He is best remembered for his operas, La Travata, and Aida. Rigoletto, with the famous 'Drinking Song.' More – La Donna E Mobile. Plus Lacaladi seta overture, 'The Silken ladder!

Next there is Leo Delibes. Best remember for 'Clare Delune.

Gioachinpo Rossni an Italian was born in Persaro, started his musical education at the very early age of six! He is most famous for is operatic overtures which are so very vibrant in style, and are programed to whet the appetite of his audiences! The overture to the Barber of Saville and many others. While loitering in Italy, let us have a rest and listen to YOU TUBE, as we should always have it available 24 hours a day. Very beautiful, and stunning collections of a heavenly musical lift to the seventh Heaven. What about that for praise! It's 'Romance in Venice!'

Antonio Vivaldi's most well-remembered work is The Four Seasons. I prefer his composition the concerto for two mandolins.

Claude Debussy was a contemporary of Maurice Ravel, both most prominent in the Impressionist style of classical music.

He was born in France in 1862, and trained at the Paris Conservatory. Clare de Lune is his possible most well-known and highly regarded composition.

Hector Berlioze a French man composed the symphony Fantastique. This work has a most triumphal finally, like Tchaikovsky's 1812 overture.

Turning to violin music, the greatest exponent of this art must be Niccolo Paganini, 1782 -1840. He was a most famous exponent of the violin ever! He enraptured his admiring audiences by the trickery of courting disaster by cutting nearly through each of his violins strings except one. As he played the spell-bound audience watched in horror as the string on his violin broke one after the other. He then continued to enthral them by a triumphal completion with his great musicianship! My favorite is his violin concerto No 1.

Georg Bizet's most memorable composition is the well-loved opera Carmen. However things are often not at all straight forward as you would suppose, as the opera was never appreciated in his life-time!

Writing about operas, what about Giacomo Puccini? He was born in 1924, and is considered to be the greatest composers of Italian opera after Verdi! My favourite is Madama Butturfly, with the stunningly beautiful aria the Humming Corus. Others that come to my mind are La boheme, 1904. Tosca,1900.

Pietro Mascagni most well-known work is Cavalier rustic Ana. It is a truly haunting and memorable composition indeed, and is frequently performed even today.

Samuel Wesley was the elder brother of the famous non-conformist preacher John Wesley. John was an Anglican clergyman, who became disillusioned with the Established church of his day. He rode around on horseback preaching his own brand of Christianity very widely, in the West Country, particularly in Cornwall.

He is well remembered for his very great contribution to Hymns which are still sung today. His brother Samuel contributed to John's evangelical passion by adding the music to his brother's great poetry. At about that time the Act of Uniformity came into law. New churches were restricted to be at least seven miles from an Anglican church. This a very misguided attempt to control and stop many attempts to reform the Anglican church, and outlaw breakaway churches springing up in competition with the state established church. Theology and with religion in general has always suffered with the malaise of many interpretations of the Holy Bible.

While on the subject of classic hymns, Hubert Parry's great music to the hymn Jerusalem, 'In England's Green and pleasant land, and not to forgetting the contrast of the 'Dark satanic mills!

You may be confused with the number of composers who are known as Barch?

However the answer is that there were three brothers, all exceptional composers. The eldest, and most widely known is Johann Sabastian Barch, followed by the younger Johann Christian Barch, and finally the baby Barch, Carle Phillip Emanuel Barch. Memorable compositions include, 'Where sheep may safely graze.' Violin Partita No.3 'Air on a G string.'

The same problem occurs with the Hydens! The eldest and most well-known is Joseph Hyden, followed by his younger brother, Michael Hyden. Joseph Hyden was not in the very least an ideal man! He composed a record-breaking number of symphonies, over 100! Favourites are symphony No. 94, 'The surprise.' No. 100, the Military. Finally No. 101, the much loved symphony called 'The Clock Symphony'.

One a listen you will understand how it acquired this nick-name! Michael Hyden was less busy apparently in his life. One memorable composition is the Cello concerto No. 2.

Going northwards to Scandinavia Finland's most famous son must be Sibelius. During the assault on his beloved homeland he composed 'Finlandia.' His countrymen were enthused by this rallying call for their beloved countries integrity and independence. Also, the work the 'Caralea' suite.

There have been some strong contenders for the top place in compositions for the violin, which has always remained with Paganini. It is quite a recent composer, Christian Friedrich Bruch, 1838 – 1900. A romantic composer, from Germany. Often played, and often very near the top of any poll of classical music is his violin concerto No. 1.

Johannes Brahms a German, there are so very many great German musicians aren't there? He was born in Hamburg in 1833 and died in 1897. He is well-known for his collection of Hungarian Dances. Other works that I very much enjoy is his Lullaby for the piano. It is bound to sooth the most restless baby!

Just a very brief mention of Sergei Prohofiev. I am not so very familiar with his compositions; however he is regarded as one of the greatest composers of the 20thcentury! I have heard his music for

Romeo and Juliet, and his Dance of the nights.

Bedrich Smetner, 1824 – 1884, a Czech citizen well remembered for the 'Bartered Bride.'

Sergei Rachmaninoff, 1873 – 1943. A composer, and pianist. Also a conductor. His Symphonic Dances, Op.45, come to my mind.

Gabriel Faure, a French composer, remembered with great affection for his work the 'Pavane.' In F – sharp minor Op. 50. This was originally for the piano, but is better known today in an orchestral arrangement with the option of a chorus accompliment. It was composed in 1887.

Offenbach, famous for his musical composition used in the dance halls of the 1940's, the Can – Can. In french, however it called the Cancan. Another notable composition is the opera, 'Orpheus in the Underworld.

Emile Waldteful, the Skaters Waltz is well known and much loved. I heard it first as a very small child! Also Lo mejor.

Amilcare Ponchielli's, Dance of the Hours is famous, and has some most delightful melodies.

J. F. Schneidig, 'Vor, Marsh Op. 79, is very well worth a listen.

J. F. Leitineritzer, Schutezen Marsh, is also good to hear.

CLASSICAL MUSIC ACCORDING TO MAURICE!

Scot Joplin was a very famous composer for the piano. His style was unique as he composed separate rhythms for the left hand and for the right hand. This is immortalised in the film score for the film 'Sting,' using his piece 'The Entertainer.' He was a black American. There were many other black great musical artists of different disciplines, Duke Ellington, with his famous Jazz Band. His version of 'When the saints go marching in,' is always going to be associated with him!

The American George Gershwin, a composer of some of the most beloved concert works of the 20th century. He reached his peak in the 1920's His opera 'Porgy and Bess, will never go out of date. The film, Summertime, was his creation, at least the music for the film. He dated many women, and seduced some of them. He proposed once, but never married!

Just to pause a little here while on memorable film-scores, what about Nigel Hess? 'Ladies in Lavender,' and other well-known film scores to his credit.

John Williams, a great present-day composer with many triumphant film scores to his name. Shindler's List, is an amazing film score, if there was any!

Returning to classical opera, Franz Waxman, a composer arranged what is called Georg Bizet's Carmen; his composition is called Carmen Fantasy.

Cesar Franck most evergreen composition is his version of Saint Thomas Aquinas, 'Bread of Heaven,' or 'Angelic

Bread.' the 'Panis Angelicus.' It was composed for the feast of Corpus Christi.

Turning to great film scores, as I have already pointed out Shostakovich's film score to the film the Gad fly, others that come to my mind are Max Steiner's music to the greatest film classic ever produced 'Gone With The Wind'.

John Barry film scores will never be forgotten. The John Dunbar theme from Dances with Wolves, and the film, Out of Africa!

James Horner's haunting and very beautiful composition to the film Titanic, An Ocean of dreams!

I believe that it is perfectly understandable to associate Classical

Music as the 'Bees Knees' of music. It mainly attracts the more educated and well-informed members of the general public. These well-meaning individuals attend grand concerts in often very large and prestigious halls. They sit attentively in complete silence to enjoy every note, and with great respect for the occasion!

Often these concert devotees overlook the vast array of what is all commonly referred to as Popular Music. In the late 50's something very special occurred unique in musical history! Pop Music exploded onto the music scene! The next decade or two saw an amazing blossoming of great talent, and creativity! This era of musical innovation has been handed down to every new generation! Everyone seems able to remember with great affection nearly all of the songs.

Those artists and musical performers were Bill Halley and the Comets. They were introduced to enthusiastic teenage audiences by the Saturday night essential viewing on BBC TV, The Six – Five Special. Lonnie Donegan, better known as Anthony James Donagan MBE! Memorable hits are, 'My old mans a dustman!'

America was not left behind at this incredible craze, and money-spinner! Elvis Presley emerged from the shadows to instant success, and international acclaim! His full title is, Elvis Aaron Presley. I expect most admirers do not know this. In Britain, an unknown prodigy emerged from English shadows with the unsuitable name for an emerging career in show-business, Harry Webb. We all know him with great affection, now as Sir Cliff Richard.

Alongside this Popular Music continued to flourish. Other genres were Jazz music with its origin from the Black community in the south of America. Many jazz musicians contributed to the great success of Pop music. County music, with its heart-land in the States had many great performers of this art.

Just to mention one to you, out of the many is Patsy Cline. I happen to love here famous song, 'If I could only see the world through the eyes of a child, what a wonderful world it would be! There would be no more trouble or strife, and there would be a Blue – bird in every tree! What a truly wonderful conception of a child's mind!

So there we are. I hope very much that my readers have enjoyed this long journey through musical history, and that some things have been added to your knowledge!

Many thanks and goodbye.

MY RECOLLECTIONS OF BRITISH POLITICAL LIFE SINCE 1939.

The Great War, World War 1, was meant to be the war that ended all wars. 1914 – 1918. Sadly, this was not to be the case. World War 1 was a conflict which left millions of dead, a very terrible carnage, and indiscriminate slaughter. Surprisingly there were no victors. A settlement was reached between the warring parties, which brought an end to the war.

In Britain there was a strong clamour for Germany, who started the war, to pay 'Reparations' for the loss of life, and destruction. This led to economic difficulties with their economy. Eventually Adolf Hitler, an extreme Fascist, came to power. The German people decided wrongly, that they did not want to embrace Communism, so they elected the Fascists instead.

Hitler started many years of re armaments, and quickly became the strongest country in Europe. This program of weapons production helped the economy, and brought an end to serious unemployment in the country.

In Britain, people who thought they had won the war, moved to strong acceptance of pacifism. The people had had their fill of war and bloodshed. Neville Chamberlain, the Prime minister correctly judged the mood of his countrymen, and when Germany invaded part of Poland, a country we had an alliance with, he adopted a policy of appeasement. After a meeting with Hitler in Germany Chamberlain returned, and on the steps of the aeroplane, he held up a piece of paper, and proclaimed, "Peace in our time!"

Germanys, military ambitions continued. A very dark cloud had enveloped Europe. Chamberlain resigned, and Winston Churchill came to power. I wonder what he felt at that time of the great challenge that lay before him. He was born at Blenheim Palace.

The country faced its greatest challenge ever, and a departure from divisive politics was found in forming a political coalition between all political parties. During the years after World War 1, pacifist sentiment led to a very dangerous weak military situation. Disarmament was in vogue! The only saving grace was the fighter plane the Spitfire. Hermann Goering, in charge of the German Luftwaffe Air Force, said that he wished he had British Spitfires! Winston Churchill, on the other hand, promised his countrymen, nothing but blood, toil, sweat and tears. Nevertheless the whole country rallied around him. He was a great orator and leader.

Hitler overran most of Europe, stopping at the English Channel on France's side. His invasion plans were stalled there as he lost the air Battle of Britain, thanks to the Spitfires and the brave young pilots.

Churchill eloquently said, "Never in the field of human conflict has so much been owed to so few!" Hitler then made his greatest mistake of all by invading Russia. He despised the Slaves. He had fostered the racist belief that the Arian German race were supreme, and that the German Reich would last 1000 years!

The great military power of Germany needed the U.S.A., Russia, and Britain to defeat it. Unlike the World War 1, total defeat of Germany was the ultimate plan. Hitler was in his bunker in Berlin, when he heard the fire-power of the Red Army drawing ever closer to him, he shot himself in the mouth. His mistress also killed herself. They dragged his body outside and burnt it with petrol. The Russians never have revealed what they did to Hitler's body

Churchill and Joseph Stalin the Russian leader met in Moscow to decide just how Europe would be divided up between the Victors. The Russians with their triumphant Red Army had completely taken Berlin, Germany's capital city. It was agreed that Berlin should be divided up into an American, British, French, and Russian zone. Churchill's famous remark was that an 'iron curtain' had fallen over Europe'!

The Second World War was far from over. The great military might of Japan still remained to haunt us all! In Britain there was an increasing demand to return to Party Politics. The British forces, still in Europe demanded change. The old order had to go. In the ensuing general election there was a massive victory for the Labour Party, with its leader Clement Atlee. Churchill, the saviour of his country did however win his seat. Although poles apart politically to Clement Atlee, they were said to be still great friends!

The elected Labour government embarked on a huge plan to bring the most important industries into public ownership. It will never be forgotten that they invented the National Health Service. Healthcare provision, for all irrespective of income. What a great vision that was, and quickly brought into being! This vision has been at the very heart of socialism since that time.

All 'good' things come to an end sometimes, and Labour lost the next election to the Conservatives. Sir Winston

Churchill was back in power. Later on Sir Anthony Eden took over. He had to deal with the Suez crisis. Britain and France had built, ran, and owned the Suez Canal in Egypt. It made a much shorter route for shipping. Egypt's leader, always trying to better the lot of his poor countrymen, wanted to nationalise the Canal. It was feared that the Egyptian's would not possess the necessary skills to take over and run the Canal efficiently. Britain and France, without American support launched an invasion of the Suez Canal area. It was a disastrous failure. Egypt then took over the running of the Canal with its revenue, and have continued to run it very well ever since!

Next in power in Britain was Harold MacMillan, known as 'Super Mac!' He was also known for the 'Night of the Long Knives!' He sacked half his cabinet! At Election time his war-cry was, "You have never had it so good!" When much later on Margaret Thatcher accused him of unleashing demand that led eventually to the very great problem of rampant inflation at 15%! MacMillan tried unsuccessfully to join the Common Market. General DE Gaulle Of world War fame pronounced his famous word 'Non!' He feared that if the U.K. was admitted then American influence would undermine European identity. He had not forgotten General Eisenhower's snub to him during the last war. MacMillan became ill, and was admitted to hospital with prostate gland problems. The Queen came to see him in hospital and a consultation took place between them, about who his successor should be. Sir Alek Douglas Hulme was chosen as the next Prime minister. He had given up his peerage to become a 'commoner' so his political ambitions could flourish!

Sir Alek Douglas Hulme's reign was short. He lost the next General Election. His wife remarked that it was because of his half-framed spectacles that he wore! Edward Heath came to power for the Conservative Party. He was encouraged to improve his small-talk, essential for electioneering, and the talking shop of the House of Commons! He had the electoral disadvantage of being a Batchelor, and after his death was accused of Child Sex Abuse, although this was never proved. He successfully led us into the Common Market.

For some considerable time the Trade Unions had asserted too much power. Jo Gormley of the Miner's Union had, what transpired to be a political strike. Gormley tried to deny this. The strike was solid, and led to terrible disruption. The three day week was introduced to conserve electricity reserves. The power stations were in the main coal-fired. Heath went to the country for a mandate. He lost the election to Labour. Harold Wilson a former Oxford Don came to power. He weakly settled with the Miners, saying, let's get back to work!" He held one of the first Referendums to decide if we should remain in the Common Market. His recommendation was accepted, and we stayed in. His achievement that he was most proud of was The Open University. Open to all! His wife Mary disliked the life of politics and persuaded him to retire to their hide-away bungalow on the Isles of Scilly.

James Callahan, the Chancellor of the Exchequer, was the next chosen leader. He refused to adopt all of Labour parties' policy. This included the very controversial policy of ending the unelected upper House of Lords. He presided over 15% inflation that saw many peoples savings evaporate! In order to control the matter he introduced a 5% pay freeze. This was rejected by the Trade Union movement, the government supporters, and led to The Winter of Discontent. Wide-spread industrial action followed. Even the Grave Diggers went on strike! Inflation took many more years to control. Our present 0% inflation figure was never thought at that time to be ever attainable!

Neil Kinnock, an honourable gentleman was Labour's chosen leader in opposition. His hands were tied by Labour's National Executive's policy of ridding us of our Nuclear Deterrent, Trident. Margaret Thatcher then won several Elections, one after the other, capitalizing on the countries' desire to keep Trident. Labour's emblem was a red rose bud. At one election victory Margaret Thatcher was presented with a bouquet of red roses by her supporters. What a slap in the face for poor Neil Kinnock!

The Trade Unions had not gone away. The miners, yet again, under the leadership of a militant left wing leader, Author

Scargill led an unashamed political strike to rid us of the hated right wing Margaret Thatcher. They were relying on their power to shut all the coal-fired power stations down. However even after one long year of industrial action this was not achieved. The lights never went out, and there was no three day week introduced. Margaret Thatcher defeated the Miners Union, and they had the humiliation of returning back to work empty handed. Thatcher poured salt into their wounds by destroying their jobs, with the introduction of Gas Powered generating stations.

Even Margaret Thatcher's reign came to an end. Her great mistake was the introduction of The Poll Tax, Local Authority revenue. It was widely felt to be unfair, and favouring the better of. Sir Geoffrey Howe an influential colleague and Minister advised her to step aside. She had brought John Major on in government. He was a finance Minister at the Treasury. He took over from her. He was a weak man who could not control his cabinet. He did, however introduce the popular National Lottery, and the end to Sunday Trading Laws.

The moderate, and highly successful Tony Blaire came to power for ten years. A Labour Party mile-stone! He brought peace to Northern Ireland that evaded Margaret Thatcher. His Lap-Dog relationship with President George Bush and their terrible misjudgement of the reason for the regime change. Also, the handling of the war in Iraq, particularly at the end. They both have to live with the death of hundreds of thousands of Iraqis.

Eventually Tony Blair's rule came to an end, and David Cameron, an old Etonian, with a Liberal coalition formed the new government. Cameron prospered, and won an overall majority in the House of Commons at the next election.

Due to great pressure form Euro-Sceptics on the right of the Conservative party Cameron decided to hold a referendum on Britain's membership of the EU. He campaigned passionately for a Stay vote. The British people were subjected to many threats about the dire consequences of leaving the EU, by all leading politicians. To their great credit they stood their ground and voted to leave the EU. This was largely due to the very real fear of uncontrolled immigration.

Cameron made the honourable decision of resigning. At his departing speech to the House of Commons he claimed that the achievement of which he was most proud of was the legalising of same sex marriages. Labour's leader Jeremy Corban reminded him that it was only passed with the support of Labour MP's.

Tony Blair, Labour's most successful leader told Labour MP's that if they voted for Jeremy Corban, an extreme left-winger, it would be political suicide! They had a death-wish and refused to be advised! The Tories new leader, the former Home secretary is Teresa May. She has recently been voted the most popular leader!

You are now up to date! Good bye.

THE SIMPLE SOLUTION TO POVERTY AND POPULATION EXPLOSION!

Very surprisingly nearly everyone in the developed world has enough money to live on. Some have much more than they need. There are even those who have an exorbitant amount of wealth! On the other side, in the Third World most people have pitiful incomes, with very few positions. I have seen it for myself on a visit some years ago to Nigeria. I saw a person's home consisting of a 'thatched' structure. Inside I was very shocked to discover that all that was inside was a straw mat for a bed! In our wealthy country Foreign Aid is to be reviewed with a reduction on the cards!

My humble solution to this very great and pressing problem is as follows. I am going to give helpful guidance to provide for a healthy and happy life for all on our beloved planet. For a start we can all save a great deal of money on food. I will mention many other arrears where a great deal of money can be saved.

I have found that I can have a healthy diet on just £5 a week! It consists of 32 Shredded Wheat biscuits, with 8 pints of full cream milk. 2Kg's of sugar, plus a litre of freshly squeezed orange juice for some fruit and vitamin C for health reasons. Should this very economical and adequate diet be too plain and monogamous for some, then variety, the spice of life, can be added for very little extra.

Other obvious savings are as follows. Many people own a car at very great expense, between £500 and £1000 a year. Older cars over five years are cheaper to buy but often have the need of very expensive repairs. In my home town of Cullompton in Devon I notice that there are many newish cars on the roads. Money does not seem to present any problem at all. The question that arises for me is why are there so many cars on our roads? There is the alternative of Public Transport. In Cullompton this means of travel is very well provided for. The buses are clean and comfortable. They are smooth and their engines just purr along. The double-decker buses run to the city of Exeter, 12 miles away every fifteen minutes. On the top deck in the front seats the panorama view is very impressive indeed. The huge window affords one a spectacular view of the proceeding journey and wonderful scenery. How very much better than driving a car, where it would be very dangerous to take one's eyes of the road immediately ahead. Driving today on our crowded road is nothing less than a great strain, which sometimes results in what is now known as 'Road Rage!' People have actually been killed!

Other, surplus to requirements, expenditure are foreign holidays, sometimes costing several thousands of pounds. What, I wonder do people in the

Third World, who have very little, think about that? Private Education is surely an unnecessary expenditure. What about Private Health Care? Surely our National Health Service, which is the envy of the whole world, is quite sufficient?

There is even a great area of completely unnecessary expenditure that, can you believe, causes great personal health risks! Smoking in our country which the great majority of people of all ages engage in has the very stark, and disturbing message in bold capitals on each box of cigarettes, 'SMOKING KILLS! It certainly shortens one's life expectancy by at least 10 years, plus many long years of ill health before. The expense, while completely obvious to all is enormous. Each pack of cigarettes cost about £10. Many people smoke three packs a day, 60! It would cost, surely unthinking people £200 a week. That is £10,000 a year, and a staggering possible £500,000 a year. What a wonderful new house one could buy for that without a need for a mortgage!

The Muslim religion forbids the drinking of alcohol. This is widely and effectively enforced in all Muslim countries. This was one of Mohamed's greatest contributions to society! It surely cannot be denied that alcohol consumption is the sure route of many ills in society. Surely we are not so inadequate as to find essential the need to drink alcohol to relax and to be sociable? Alcohol is directly responsible for many crimes. The breakup of good relationships, and domestic violence, so very harmful for children to witness. Like tobacco it is addictive. The great problem arises in that one cannot tell that even just one drink may lead to the very terrible affliction of alcoholism. It has, at its door the great difficulty of sexual contact, that when sober afterwards the woman often feels that she has not given her consent for sex. The difficult to prove charge of rape then ensues, with some untrue convictions of men, who are sent to prison unlawfully.

Returning to the much loved motor car. If we could persuade motorists to give up cars they don't really require, it would free up the road network for many more buses. It would spell the end to congestion, and the expensive congestion charge in major cities. With many more buses we could provide a good service even to small communities. Further I add that we could also dispense with the rail network. The High Speed link, so very expensive would really not be at all necessary.

The money saved would be unprecedented. This would enable large and very necessary funds to be diverted to the Third World. Another great and totally unforeseen benefit that has escaped the attention of all major politicians would be a great reduction in Global Warming! Thus saving our beloved planet!

MY SEQUAL TO TOM BROWN'S SCHOOL DAYS.

My readers may have read my first book called, 'Is Religious Belief Really Necessary'? My autobiography was at the end of this book. I wish now to be allowed to amplify and elaborate the early years of my life story.

Just to recap a little I was born in 1943 on a small dairy farm near the small village of Hemyock in Devon. My dear but poor parents sent me to a posh primary school where I learnt very little. This resulted in me failing the 11+ exam at the age of 11 years, and meant that I would not be selected to have an academic education at a Grammar school.

My parents decided to wangle things for me to go to a co-educational Direct-Grant Grammar school as a boarder. This was at Cheadle Hulme School, Cheshire, without taking the mandatory entrance exam which everyone realised I would fail.

The school was 250 miles away from the security of my home. I was very home sick and missed my dear mother terribly. I started my long journey to school from Taunton station, Somerset. As the steam train came to a stop at the station platform,

I marvelled at the giant steam engine with all the steam and smoke emitting from the engine. As it struggled to start pulling the carriages, the huge wheels of the engine slipped on the rails, but eventually it got up speed. We went through a very long tunnel under the Severn Estuary, A train on the opposite track passed by at speed in the darkness. It was very frightening as it only seemed to be a few inches between us.

Our first stop was in South Wales at Pontypool station. We then headed north to Hereford then Shrewsbury until we reached the great railway town of Crew. The journey to school would take seven hours to complete. The final destination would be Liverpool Lime Street station. I left before this at Stockport station, where I was met by my elder sister Pamela. She had just acquired a post at my school as a Science teacher. I then caught a local train to take me back to Cheadle Hulme station. Then I made my way on a cinder pathway to my new school.

When I had unpacked my trunk I was introduced to my Mentor a 4th form boy. I had to report to him each day. The wake-up alarm sounded at 7am in the morning. I had to dress and clean my shoes in the 'boot room'. Then I had to go on parade in the boy's playroom, to be inspected by a prefect. Next we all formed up in our tables, and then marched to the dining room on the next floor for our breakfast.

In the dining room the girls sat on one side and the boys on the other. At the head of each table was a prefect who dished out all the food. The junior boys sat at the end of the table called 'Slops'. They had to pour the tea, and pile up the dirty dishes, for the seven people on each table. After grace was said at the end of the meal the girls filled out. The boys watched them all eagerly, particularly the pretty ones! The boys then formed up at the door where the post was distributed. The prefect flicked the letters through the air to us.

I found, not to my great surprise to be in the bottom set. This was not as bad as it seems as a boy in this form became managing director of the famous accountancy firm. In the week day evenings we had two hours of home-work called 'Prep', 7pm to 9pm. One evening this boy was sitting in front of me, and he turned around to speak to me. He saw my writing effort and exclaimed, "Maurice you can't even write!"

My mother believed that my sister would mother me. However after a few first days at my new school, one day I met my sister Pamela for the first time in the playground. She exclaimed that she had not spoken to me before as I had looked so very unhappy! Later she intercepted a love note to my first ever girlfriend Angela Lauder. Pamela summoned me to her room, and accosted me with this severe rebuke, 'Maurice, you have not come to this school for this kind of thing!' Is it any wonder that I never had another girlfriend until I was 38. I did live to tell the tale!

Our House Master was a man called Mr Alek Frederick Finch. He devoted his whole life to the boys of our school. He seemed to be always working 24 hours a day! His nick name was 'Faff'! This was because his office floor was covered with what we described as 'Faff Notes!' His many reminder's for his very busy life. In the summer holidays he took several boys in several yachts to the Norfolk Broads, to learn how to sail a boat.

We had visits to The Free Trade Hall in Manchester, Lancashire. This was to introduce us to the great pleasure of Classical Music. I remember one concert with the Halle Orchestra under their conductor Sir John Barbirolli. They performed Berlioz Symphony Fantastique. I remember the percussionist, a tall gentleman standing bolt upright all the time. When, at the appropriate time he sounded the cymbals' he turned them wide open to project the sound to us. The lady, by contrast, who played the Kettle Drums, sat down when not required to play them. At the closing finally of this great symphony the brass section of the orchestra on the right side on the stage, all stood up while playing. It was a very impressive sceptical indeed to see. The hall was very large with two balconies one on top of the other. Another concert we attended was given by Duke Elliton and his Jazz Band. Their final rendition was, 'When the Saints Go Marching In!' The whole audience all clapped to the rhythm of the music.

If I may, just return to the matter of the orchestra, Andre Rieu and his Johann Strauss Orchestra and Choir, has enthralled millions of devotes around the world, with his unique brand of tuneful classical melodies. He is a great Showman, leading his orchestra from the front from his violin. A feature of his concerts, all over the world, is the audience participation. They even sing along to some of their classical favourites! Andre Rieu, a Dutch man says that it gives him enormous pleasure to bring so much pleasure and happiness to our troubled world. He rightly claims that good music is healing, and mentally healthy! The Italian Niccolo Paganini, an Italian gentleman and composer, 1782-1840, is famous for being the most accomplished violin virtuoso of all time! He entranced his audience by cutting nearly through all of his violin's strings except one. As he played each string broke in turn until he was only left with one string! He continued miraculously to the end of his music score! Even Andre Rieu is having trouble in emulating Paganini!

We played games around our boarding house. One was in the darkness a tin can was kicked a long way, and we all had to run and hide in the bushes. Even 5th formers joined in with the lower forms. We had to try and return without being caught. We had three aside indoor football tournaments in the boy's playroom. We all enjoyed playing. In the 5th form common room we had a billiard table, and a tournament was arranged for all the boys.

There were about 80 boys and girls in the boarding house. In the winter evening we has film shows in the girl's playroom. The Lady Killers, starring Alek Guinness.

It was a tale about robbery with a classical music twist! The gang of robbers rented an upstairs room in a house of an elderly lady. They had the novel idea of hiding their ill-gotten gains in the cases of musical instruments like that of Chellos and Double Bases. They hoodwinked the lady, by playing on a gramophone a record of Boccherini's Minuet in E. I remember what a very great impression this melody had on me. It is often played today on Classic FM radio.

At the film shows Mr Finch used to play the starter cartoon film backwards as he found it so amusing. Hobson's -Choice was a very memorable film, starring that great character actor Charles Laughton. A seemingly ugly man with a large belly! John Mills another great character actor who was Laughton's cobbler, confined to an underfloor workshop beneath the shoe shop floor. A wealthy lady who was a valid customer asked to meet the workman who made such good boots. Mills emerged from a trap door in the floor to be congratulated. After some considerable time, Mills met and married the boss's daughter. They were extremely poor and only afforded a brass wedding ring to always remind them of their humble start in life together. The rich lady lent them the money to set up a rival shoe shop in competition with his former boss. They eventually were so successful that they drove Laughton out of business, and even took over his shop. Charles Laughton starred in the movie, 'The Hunch-Back of Notre Dame', complete with scary bats in the belfry! It seems that male actors can get away without good looks, but actresses have to be stunningly beautiful!

Another classic film we were treated to was Charles Dickens's, Oliver Twist. This boy is famous for asking for more! The wheelie character, called Fagin corrupted poor boys to become pick-pockets. There was Bill Sykes a grownup thief who had a small but faithful dog who followed him everywhere, even though Sykes ill-treated the dog.

Returning to night time in the boarding house, the girls dormitories were a short corridor away from the boys. There was a door between but it was never locked. The twain never met! The girls and boys spent a lot of time together, but I never heard of one girl getting pregnant!

With the day pupils and boarders, who always felt the school belonged to them, amounted to a total of 750 pupils. This required there to be two lunch time sittings in our large dining room. I remember the clatter and din of the metal lids of the food containers being dropped on the floor, immediately after the silence required for grace to be said.

My home town of Cullompton, Devon, with a population of 8000, has still not raised the required amount of money for an indoor heated swimming pool. At my privileged school, a former very rich pupil donated a marvellous indoor heated swimming pool. It was quite large, and was reputed to be the best quality building for miles around! It was heated by a coal-fired boiler 24 hours a day, 365 days a year. The water and air was always very warm, even when it was snowing outside! The water was even too hot sometimes for serious swimming. Every Saturday afternoon the boys and girls, separately, had an hour in the pool. There was as usual a shallow end, and a deep end with diving boards, and a spring board. Sometimes for utter devilment we took off from the highest diving board and bomb-shelled with a great splash to drench the supervising teacher! Boys will be boys!

On a more serious note I propose to now focus on work, lessons and possible learning. We had only one or two really good teachers that I could relate to and learn from. I had been born with a peculiar brain that could only understand lessons, when what was being taught had to be put in a very simple and logical form, with complete silence in the classroom. Two examples I will give of these two extremes. Mr Neil, a French teacher was completely useless at classroom control. He should have been sacked long ago, as all bad teachers should be today. I have a strong feeling that all bad teachers in our schools, and there are many, should be summarily dismissed. My maths teacher, Mrs Becroft in our algebra lessons, at the beginning failed to point out that $x=2b+4qw$, that x stood for the unknown quantity. This simple omission puzzled me for ages! The other side of the coin was my best ever teacher, our overworked House master Mr Finch. In my final 5th year he prepared us for our 'O' Level exam in June 1959. He taught us the quite hard subject Chemistry. The irony of this was that he was an Oxford History graduate and knew nothing at all about academic Chemistry. He found time, that he did not possess, to learn up each lesson that he gave us. He did a lot of demonstrations in the front of the class, although he was rather nervous of experiments with things like solid Sodium, which has to be kept under oil, as contact with the air and more importantly water makes it burst into flames! As a born teacher with the gift of clarity in explaining difficult concepts, he excelled brilliantly! The result was not just in the eating but in my attainment of a pass with a mark of 65%! I managed a pass mark, with a not so good teacher, called Mr Baker, in Physics of 45%. I think that Physics is harder even than Chemistry. Girls shy away from it!

Our Library was not well stocked with good books, but all was not lost. We had all the daily newspapers to read in the Library, and also in our common rooms where we had more newspapers, separately for each year. The Library was stocked with many periodicals like Newsweek, Time Magazine, The Spectator, The Amateur Photographer, and so on.

For games we played Rugby in the Autumn Term, Lacrosse in the Spring Term, and of course Cricket in the Summer Term. I was never good a sport like my dear son Samuel, who at only 18 plays Rugby for Devon County. I did play Lacrosse for a junior team as a goalie. It is widely thought that Lacrosse is a girl's Public School game, but in the North West of England, especially in Cheshire and Lancashire it is a boys and man's rough game. The goal keeper has a wire mast covering his face, and chest padding, as the ball, the weight and size of a cricket ball which could seriously injure you. Padded gloves for the hands like wicket keepers wear were a necessity. The Lacrosse racket is rather like David's sling hurling a stone that hit and sank into Goliath's forehead. The rest of the Bible story is that David then used Goliath's sword to cut his head off. He then proceeded to exalt himself in front of his fellow countrymen, on the other side of the valley, who were too afraid to fight the Philistines, and their champion Goliath, by holding Goliath's head aloft!

Because of the rather large number of boys in the boarding house, the Scouts were divided into two Troops. We had a

Scout Hut on our campus. I was in the patrol led by a boy called John Tidwell. At the close of the meeting we formed up in rows of each of six patrols, and stood to attention, while a short prayer was uttered by the Scout Leader Mr Smith. The latter was a slightly effeminate gentleman, known as RAS. When supervising tea in the dining room, there was a disturbance. He stood up at the supervisor's table with a lady teacher in charge of the girls, by his side. RAS went red in the face, with all the rage he could muster.

Our Headmaster was a man called Mr D. H. Whiting O.B.E. He was awarded this great honour for his services to education while living in Egypt. He made the time, which no other Head does today, to write a line or two at the bottom of 750 pupil's end of term reports. He also kept in his vast memory, a working knowledge of each pupil under his care, so that he would be confident enough to write a leaving Testimonial. On mine he was kind enough to recognise that I had been well-liked in the boarding house, and was a well-mannered boy. That is all my dear parents required of me. They never ever made any negative comments about my academic failure. They must have loved me so very much! They found it a real struggle to pay my school fees.

Sundays in the boarding House, in the morning we marched in small groups to our own particular denomination. I went to a Methodist Church, where we sat out of the way in the balcony. The Minister always gave us a special talk just for us,

One time he told a story of a boy, who when asked to go to his Headmaster's study, took the precaution of closing the head's door behind him. I have never forgotten this example of good manners! The evening service was held in the Dining room. As always, the girls sat on one side, and the boys on the other. Enforced separation! We all enjoyed singing the classic hymns. One line of a famous hymn goes like this, 'to follow duly.' There was a popular girl called Julie, so when we got to the word duly, all the boys sang the name Julie instead! Her face went bright red with embarrassment! Sometimes the evening service was taken by the 6th form. They were poor, when it came to theology! As a direct result they got out of their difficulty, by hiring Faith and Fact films, instead of the difficulty of preaching. One was on the Honey Bee. They have a remarkably ordered society in the insect world. My father kept bees in several hives. He would approach them gingerly, with a smoke generator, which seem to anesthetise the disturbed and very angry bees. My father wore a hat with a net over his face for protection from bee stings. Bees are somewhat like Islamic State terrorists, they die after just one sting. The stolen honey was in wax frames, several in one section. The frames had a wax middle on which the bees built their geometric wax containers, hexagon in shape and constructed at an angle, so that the liquid honey would not spill out. They laboriously travelled long distances to search for pollen from flowers, collecting it on their six legs. They had a wonderful sense of direction, as they always found their way back to their hive. The frames of honey were assembled into a hand driven centrifuge which rotated very quickly forcing the honey from the honey combs. The extracted honey was then put into another container and filtered through fine net gauze to filter out any wax comb. It was then left to ripen and mature. It was then still runny, but later on it always crystalizes. We put it in labelled jars and took it to a lovely seaside town called Sidmouth. The bees, with their hard to produce honey, which greedy man had stolen from them, were fed on sugar during the long wintertime. Bees are incredibly clean and fastidious creatures!

One of my school's big events was the school play. It was such a triumph, helped by the 6th former's who stayed on for a 3rd year waiting for a place at university. It was sometimes written up in the Manchester Guardian Newspaper. This later became the national newspaper called The Guardian. In addition the 5th form boys had to produce a play including lower form pupils. One play for each of the school's four Houses.

A boy who had been expelled from his former school, was given a last chance at our school. He was always in trouble for smoking. This was not allowed at our school. One day he invited me to break-bounds and go for a drink at a local pub. On the way back we were spotted, and reported. I was caned twice. He was severely beaten with a cane, and summarily expelled. I believe he became a reporter with a local newspaper. Why this all happened is the purpose of me recounting this story to you. When he realized that the game was up, he said to me, "Maurice I will say that I went with you to buy some cigarettes. You will not get into so much trouble then." He must have known that in considering me, he would get into much more trouble, through buying cigarettes than alcohol!

Will you allow me to pause here, and to digress? I wish to share with you some of my memorable films and TV series of the distant past. Steptoe and Son, this starred Wilfred Bramble and Harry H. Courbet. This was a long running series, which started out in life a single episode. The elderly father Albert, always got the better of his gawky accident prone son Harold, who was always trying unsuccessfully to climb up from the bottom rung of society's ladder!

The 'Black and White Minstrels Show' was a compulsory Saturday's evening entertainment. I loved the beautiful girls with their very elaborate costumes, which their blackened faced male dancing parkers never seemed to mark the girl's beautiful dresses. This show would today be deemed to be too politically incorrect! Another classic, long running TV series with the same problem today, was Coronation Street. Annie Walker the Land Lady of The Rover's Return Pub. A middle class lady of a very superior air exchanged a dialogue with Hilda Ogden the cleaner at the Pub. She was attired in a smock with her hair done up in curlers covered with a head scarf, and leaning on her broom with a bent cigarette in her mouth. Their class warfare exchanges were so very amusing, and entertaining. Why they would be considered offensive today is hard to understand.

Turning to comedy, if I may, Frankie Howard I recall with great affection. He was a blatant homosexual who could contort his face in a myriad of different ways. He would amuse us by gawping at ladies boobs! The 'Carry On' films were a great success. Kenneth Williams with is nasals voice, another homosexual, Sid James, Hattie Jakes, and Barbara Winsor, a buxom lady always willing to return sexist remarks, and not forgetting Bernard Breslau; this long series of films were at a time when sexual humour, innuendo, and remarks were thought to be way out of court. These films flourished on sexual innuendoes, that everyone enjoyed them, and took it all in good humour.

Do you agree with me that if you were asked what is your most memorable, and very old classical film, I guess you might say 'Gone with the Wind?' Clark Gable and Janet Leigh. Gable was such an amorous lover, and even a great cad he was with his black twirled moustache! Their interaction during the courtship was so very strident, rather like William Shakespeare's, 'Taming of the Shrew. 'With Richard Burton, and Elizabeth Taylor. The film score by Max Steiner called 'Tara's Theme.'

Turning again to America that seems to be the home of classic films, what about, 'Destry Rides Again.' James Stewart, with his famous drawling voice, which went so very well with his American accent. In the black and white film the rich and powerful villain of the wild-west town, in order to secure his powerful base, hired the town drunk to be the next town Sherif. As is sometimes the case, all is not as certain as expected. The new Sherif decided to go dry and sober up. He got in touch with James Destry who was renowned for his accurate sharp-shooting. On arriving in the town the Sherif was dismayed to find that Destry had arrived without his guns. He strangely decided not to use or carry guns. Reluctantly the Sherif made him Deputy Sherif. One day a posse of Mexicans on horse-back rode into town firing their guns indiscriminately. The women in the street fled for their safety. As they approached Destry they drew up and stopped. Destry accosted them in a mild way, and requested to examine their guns. They snubbed him by handing two guns to him, and remarking that he probably would not know how to use them. Across the road was a tall building with a roof with several small decorative knobs. He took aim and with each shot blew of each knob! The Mexicans fled jumping on their horses, and rode out of town the same way as they had arrived at great speed!

This classic, and very long and expensive epic, with thousands of extras, 'Ben Hur'. starring Charlton Heston a man of magnificent physique. It was set in the time of Jesus Christ in Palestine. The most clever film director showed Jesus, only twice in the long film from the back view, never revealing His face. This enabled the viewers to keep their preconceived image of their Lord intact. There was the famous chariot race with Ben Hur competing with the occupying Roman Tribune. Ben Hur had beautiful white Arab horses, while his black-haired opponent had matching black horses. Black is synonymous with evil!

Boris Pasternak's Nobel Prize winning novel called Dr Zhivago was made into yet another classic and memorable movie. Omar Sharif, Egypt's most famous son, and Julie Christie. What a brilliant actress she was. She played a part as a young beautiful and sensual girl, and through the long years to a mature lady, 'Laura.' The villain Rod Steiger known as Komerovsky touched Laura's pouted lips with one finger of his hand, and unkindly remarked to her that she need not claim rape, as you know you wanted it! Uri Zhivago's wife, Geraldine Chaplin, Tonya, a beautiful girl. Sir Ralf Richardson as Yuri's adopted father. His daughter became Yri's wife. His mistress Laura and evil Komerosky had a girl played by Rita Tushingham.

The film 'Sting' featured the musician Scot Joplin and his piano piece, The Entertainer' Scot Joplin composed a unique style of piano music with different rhythms for the left hand and the right hand. He was a black American.

Ryan's Daughter, with Robert Mitchum usually playing a matshow part, but this time a wimp who could not consummate his marriage to the very beautiful Sarah Miles. John Mills played a brilliant character of a mentally retarded man. The Roman Catholic Priest was also very convincing. Sarah asked him one day, "Is their not more to marriage?" He replied, "What do expect Rosy?" The film gave a great insight into the insuperable problems of Ireland, the reason for the rise of the IRA.

Titanic, a more recent block-buster starred Leonardo Dicaprio and the emerging super-star Kate Winslet. She delighted male viewers by baring all! The music, by James Horner was a real delight. The piece named, 'Ocean of Dreams.' A haunting melody, accompanied by a wordless soprano voice!

Dancing with Wolves is remembered more for the music than the story by Kevin

Costner. It was composed by John Barry, 'The John Dunbar Theme.'

Lastly I recall taking my dear mother to the ABC cinema in Exeter to see quite a young but very famous Cliff Richard, formally Harry Webb! What a great entertainer he is. The unknown superstar Olivia Newton-John was the female back-up. The film Grease starred her with John Travolta. Once at Wimbledon Centre Court when rain stopped play, Cliff a tennis enthusiast, when rain stopped play, he entertained the crowd with his many hit songs. Everyone joined in with the words everyone knew so well!

In drawing to a close, after this trip down memory lane, may I end by saying a big, heart-felt thank you to all those brilliant people in the Arts, Music, and Literature who have all enriched our lives so very greatly!

Thank you and good bye.

A TREMENDOUS TRIUMPH OVER GREAT ADVERSITY

My home was extremely simple. I was born to very poor but dear parents at a nursing home at Wellington, Somerset, UK. We managed without any main services like mains water and electricity. We pumped water from a well which never dried up during the summer time. Rural electricity only became available many years later. My parents rented a small dairy farm of 70 acres. This was near the village of Hemyock in Devon.

Although poor my parents were very virtuous indeed and completely unselfish in every possible way. Their way of prudent, and very careful living, made it possible for them to save a lot of money for their five children. They also had the great insight to recognise the importance of giving their children a very sound education. This policy paid off as my elder brother became multi-millionaire, and my sister, although from a very isolated small village became a Doctor. I was sent to a posh private primary school where I learnt very little and failed my 11+ exam at the age of 11 years. The reason why my parents chose this type of school was to try and prevent me socialising with unbelievers. The Gentiles as the Bible so aptly put it. In order to prevent me from having a non-academic education at a Secondary Modern School, where they believed I would only be fitted to become a 'Hewer of Wood and a Drawer of Water'! My parents although religious wangled things to achieve my acceptance as a boarder at a co-educational direct grant grammar school, without sitting the mandatory entrance examination, which everyone expected me to fail.

I was sent off to my new secondary school on a 250 mile train journey to Cheadle Hulme School, in Cheshire. That first night I found myself in a dormitory of 40 boys I had never met before. Unwisely my mother had made me promise to kneel down by my bed to say my prayers to God. I looked around to see if any of the boys were doing the same. No one did so I was too afraid to. I went to sleep sobbing because I had broken my promise to my dear mother.

My education was nevertheless quite rewarding. I had a very good social education indeed. I mixed with some clever children from good backgrounds. We all seemed to acquire girlfriends, but they quickly gave me up, as I was immature at love making. We had dances in our large dining room, sometimes with a live band. I liked the Barn Dance. We formed two large concentric circles, one of boys and the other of girls. We rotated with the music meeting the next girl and so on. The girls had their best frocks on, and we had a short dance and chat with each girl. I thought this was very civilised indeed.

I was introduced to music by my mother, who in spite of poverty purchased a new piano from a firm called Duck, Son and Pinker in Bath, Avon. She learnt to play a piece of piano music called The Maiden's Prayer. I loved the melody and all the fast high notes played by the right hand. At school we had trips to The Free Trade Hall in Manchester. We heard the Halle Orchestra under the direction of Sir John Barbirolli. Also we saw a lecture and slide show given by Sir Vivian Foulk's expedition to the South Pole. During the summer holidays we went sailing on the Norfolk Broads. We also had 15 mile hikes in the Pennine Hills.

At the age of 15 I left school with only two 'O' Levels, Physics and Chemistry although they were hard subjects. I only managed 20% at English Language. I experienced great difficulty with writing and spelling. I was not however dyslexic as I could read quite well. In the year of 1959 I came back home to manage my parents farm as my father was very ill. I found this was something I could at last manage, and I quite enjoyed it. I was interested in breeding cows with an increased milk yield, sometimes they would give six gallons a day, that's 48 pints to you and me! The cows were artificially inseminated as a bull was thought to be too dangerous. The farm was eventually sold as my parents needed the money tied up in the farm to retire in some modest luxury.

The farm sale was a success. The Estate Agent Mr Carter said he would give me a good reference. My parents gave me all the money raised by the sale of the Live and Dead stock, for my giving up the chance to own the farm one day in the future. It enabled me to by my first home in Tiverton in Devon.

I applied for a job as a Laboratory Technician in a school in Crediton in Devon. I was given a Day Release' by my school to study at Exeter College in Devon, where I passed with credit a City and Guilds exam. My lecturers felt that I was a promising student, so they arranged for me to have an interview with the Principal of St. Luke's teacher training College in Exeter. After my first year there I had to do six weeks of teaching practise at Queen Elizabeth's Grammar School in Crediton. I enjoyed this experience and felt I was good at explaining things to young children. I once had some liquid nitrogen boiling at many degrees below freezing. Liquid oxygen is light blue in colour, nitrogen is clear. One can do very interesting experiments with the super cold liquid nitrogen. No one at the school had ever seen liquid air before. I acquired it from Exeter University before lessons started on that day.

I left St. Luke's which is now part of Exeter University, as I was in great difficulty with my first main subject Chemistry. The reason was that I had not done it at A level, and my course was post A Level. My leaving reference from the Principal was very good indeed. Mr. J. P. Smeal M A Cantab. J. P. He was a very stern gentleman, but he wrote that my colleagues and I formed a very high opinion of Mr. Stevens as a man. He could not have paid me a greater compliment, even though I failed. He continued that at teaching practice I proved capable and confident, preparing my lessons with care, and that I received good reports from my Headmaster. He ended with these words, "I confidently support Mr. Stevens's application for any suitable post." A senior lecturer wrote to me after I left saying that if he had known that I was thinking of leaving he would never have let me. I then applied for a post of Senior Laboratory Technician at Sherborn Public School, Dorset. I was given a greater salary than I asked for plus a good ground floor furnished flat for a peppercorn rent of £2.50 a week. One afternoon a physics master who I worked for asked me if I would like to come and share his 'scrambled eggs'! When I arrived at his posh home I was taken aback as his wife had gone to great lengths to prepare a very elaborate meal for me. I took this to be the greatest act of kindness in an invitation that I was ever going to receive in all my life!

I was however a very lonely man. I became very ill with schizophrenia. I lost my job at Sherborn school but they gave me a good reference that enabled me to get the same post at Tiverton Grammar School in Devon. The Council wanted a medical report from my G P as the job was pensionable. My Doctor said he would have to lie to the Council about my medication that I was on for the rest of my life as I would never be able to get a job if he did not. One day a physics teacher Mr. Hunneyball asked me to give his class of 4th formers a talk on international phone dialling. The class looked very miserable but heard me in complete silence. As I left the class room I was startled as the class all broke out into a round of applause. I have never known a class clap a teacher before.

At the age of 38 I still was without a girlfriend. I was so afraid of girls. On holiday with my nephew John a Doctor, in Tenerife. I met Marie-Therese a French girl about 22. She was exceptionally beautiful, and spoke perfect English. Her profession was as a Concert Pianist. She had recently been going out with an Air Line pilot who had been killed in a car crash. She asked me out. In her first letter to me she said she had spent a very good evening with me, with my blue eyes and tender hands. And that I was most successful. I just could not believe it. She ended her letter with these words, "With tenderness" which impressed me greatly. The following summer she invited me to join her on holiday in Saint-Tropez. We never went to bed again in all of the ten years of our relationship. However after her shower in the morning she asked me each time to put my arms around her, and smell her expensive Joy perfume. I gradually lost my fear of being intimate with girls. I will always love her for helping me. I would have never been able to meet my wife, or to have fathered a child without her help.

Just before our relationship ended I met my wife. She was only 17 when she asked me out. I was an old 46! We courted for five long years when she asked me to marry her. We were married for six years and had a planned baby called Samuel. He is now 18 and very gifted. He wants to become a Doctor.

When Samuel was only two and a half, my wife and I separated. She took Samuel with her. She was a Detective Sargent at that time. It was a terrible wrench for me as I had bonded with Samuel. I had been a full-time house-husband, and had looked after him all the time.

After my divorce I was very depressed, partly because I had an underactive thyroid. When at last this was addressed by my GP I was much better. I then made the terrible mistake of suddenly stopping my medication, and I became seriously ill. My very tidy home became like a pig sty. I was again sectioned and locked up in a

Mental Hospital for several months. During this time I was abused by some of the staff. The Chief Executive of the Hospital trust upheld my complaints but took no action against his staff.

In my stay in hospital I was befriended by the Consultant Psychiatrist. One day he said to me that he had made an important discovery, that the real reason why I was so clever even though I had read very little in my life, was because I was very sensitive and observant with a remarkable photographic memory.

I wish to emphasise to my readers that my life at 73 years is now very wonderful. During the seven years of not seeing Samuel he wrote me 60 letters ending, "Lots of love, Samuel, XXXX!"

The true story of my life consists of tragedy, suffering, hope, joy, love, and even sex! It is indeed a story of a tremendous triumph over great adversity! On closing on a lighter note, one of my best jokes is, the Chancellor of the Exchequer in his budget speech to the House of Commons told this very amusing joke, he said that Labour's economic policy was like Dolly Parton. An incredible figure without any visible means of support!

SECOND THOUGHTS!

I like the old adage 'Think Big'! Just as an afterthought this is what I propose to do to end my book. I wish to be bold enough to suggest a possible solution to the terrible problem that confronts the whole of our world, Islamic State! Leading politicians have so far not come up with an answer. What is done, is just to kill the terrorists. However just as you kill them more pop up! They threaten the whole stability of the world.

Let us consider recent history for a possible solution, South Africa and Northern Ireland. Both presented an insuperable problem, which most people believed would never be solved. Everyone thought bloodshed was inevitable for the problem of South Africa. The white minority imprisoned Nelson Mandela in a terrible island prison, for 27 years. His career as a brilliant Lawyer was shattered. His health was compromised. How did he manage to keep his mind, body and soul intact?

President De Clerk made a very bold move in releasing Mandela from jail. They engaged in two years of negotiation, which ended in a peaceful transfer of power to the black majority. Mandela could have decided that the very human position of seeking revenge for the terrible injustice that had befallen him at the hand of the white minority. Mandela showed the whole world the tremendous power of forgiveness. What a very great man in putting his country before his feelings, and the vision of a united country for all its people as equals!

Northern Ireland had 30 years of strife, killings and religious hatred. There seemed to be no solution. Margret Thatcher refused to negotiate with so called terrorists. Tony Blair a moderate politician decided wisely to enter into talks with the IRA. This led to the Good Friday agreement. The IRA did not achieve what they had been fighting for so long, a United Ireland. They compromised. Did you ever think that terrorists would do that? They settled for power sharing, with Martin McGuinness a former commander in the IRA becoming deputy First Minister. Even the Queen has shaken hands with him! Peace between the warring two communities is now solid!

We can now see that the impossible can become a great reality. So, rather than not knowing what to do about Islamic State, let us try to enter into a dialogue with them, showing them a better way of life, in offering them forgiveness, and understanding, particularly of their grievances.

As Muslims they would accept Jesus as a prophet, one of the greatest men to have ever lived. On the cross Jesus said of the men who crucified Him, "Father, forgive them for they know not what they do"! Nelson Mandela followed in Jesus's foot- steps!

Good bye!

MY LIFE'S MEMORIES

My son Samuel with his Duke of Edinburgh Bronze Award

My son playing rugby

My married home and back garden with my wife and Labrador Lily

The back garden

My favorite photo of my son Samuel

My wife to be and myself on holiday in Greece

My lounge where I live now after my divorce.

My wedding photo.

More wedding photo.

All my family at my wedding reception.

My wife, child and dog Lily at the seaside.

My beautiful wife and dear son Samuel.

Before I was married as a bachelor with my Aunties.

My son with our Labrador

My young son Samuel after
my amicable divorce.

Samuel asleep with his Beatrix Potter bunny.

Sunrise through the trees near my home in Cullompton, Devon.

Knightshayes Court, Tiverton, Devon.

Samuel on his Duke of Edinburgh Award hike on Dartmoor, Devon

Samuel in France eating raw oysters.

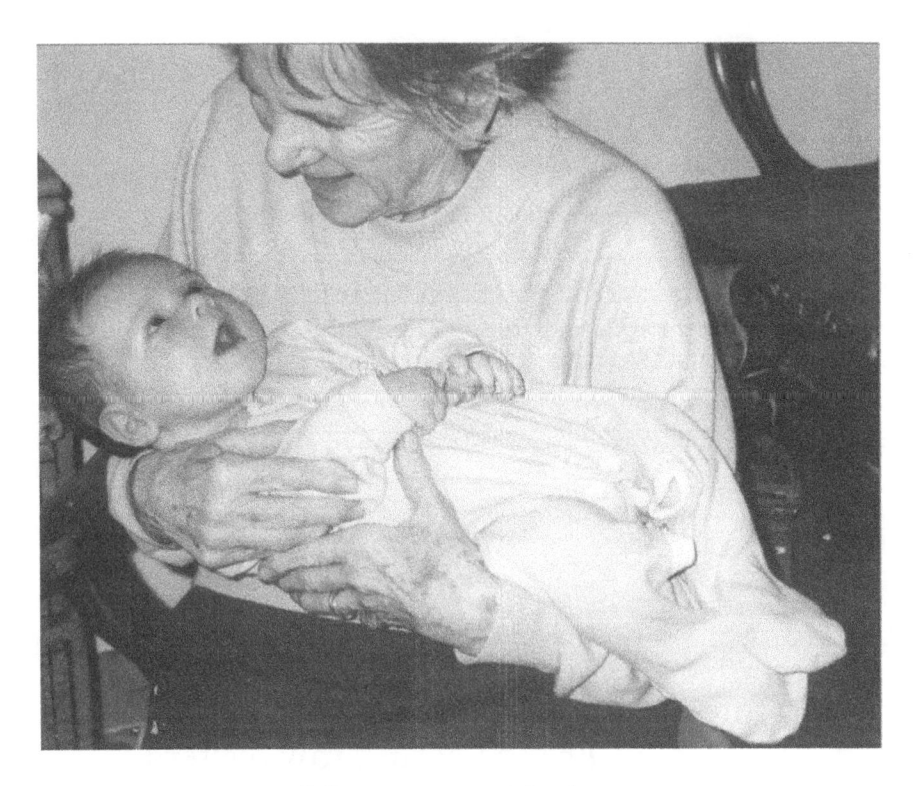

My son as a baby.

My very dear mother Mary.

When I was young and handsome at the age of 38 on holiday in Saint-Tropez.

Flowers.

The pond at Knightshayes Court.

Knightshayes Court.

Winter near my home in Cullompton, Devon.

A bird nearby.

My photo.

BIBLE STORY REFERENCE:

The story of Joseph - Genesis Chapter 37

The Good Samaritan - Luke 10 v 25.

The Woman Taken In Adultery - John 8 v 3.

Mary Madeleine - Luke 7 v 36.

God the Father, God of Love - John 3 v 16. 96

Maurice J. G. Stevens

Noah - Genesis - 6 to 10.

Canaan Land of Milk and Honey - Exodus 3 v 16.

Virgin Birth - Luke 1 v 26 to 38.

The Resurrection - Mark 16 v 1 to 8.

The Ascension - Matthew - 28 v 16 to 20.

The Upper Room - John 20 v 19 to 30.

mauricejgstevens@gmail.com

Lightning Source UK Ltd.
Milton Keynes UK
UKHW01f1949180718
325933UK00001B/78/P